Tc
Lo

CH00868972

P.E.N.
New Poetry I

In the same series:

P.E.N. New Fiction I
edited by Peter Ackroyd

P.E.N.
New Poetry I

Edited by Robert Nye

QUARTET BOOKS
London   Melbourne   New York

First published by Quartet Books Limited 1986
A member of the Namara Group
27/29 Goodge Street
London W1F 1PD

All rights reserved

Introduction copyright © Robert Nye

Poems copyright © Dannie Abse; Peter Ackroyd; John
Ash; John Ashbery; Elizabeth Baines; George Barker; Alan
Bold; D. Brennan; Stanley Cook; Neil Curry; Gloria Evans
Davies; Dick Davis; Cozette de Charmoy; Carol Ann Duffy;
Gavin Ewart; Alastair Fowler; Geoffrey Grigson; Tony
Harrison; Philip Hobsbaum; Michael Hofmann; Michael
Horovitz; Anthony Howell; Michael Hoyland; Jenny
Joseph; P.J. Kavanagh; Jean Hanff Korelitz; B.C. Leale;
Christopher Logue; George MacBeth; Norman MacCaig;
Joan McGavin; Angus Martin; Tomas O Canainn; Stephen
Plaice; Sacha Rabinovitch; Simon Rae; Peter Redgrove; Sue
Roe; Peter Russell; Vernon Scannell; Martin Seymour-
Smith; W.G. Shepherd; Penelope Shuttle; C.H. Sisson; Iain
Crichton Smith; Derek Stanford; Gillian Stone; Stefan
Themerson; John Wakeman; John Welch; Robert Wells;
Hugo Williams; Jane Wilson; David Wright

This book has been published with financial assistance from
the Arts Council of Great Britain

British Library Cataloguing in Publication Data

P.E.N. new poetry I.
1. English poetry – 20th century
I. Nye, Robert
821'.914'08   PR1225

ISBN 0–7043–2565–9

Typeset by MC Typeset, Chatham, Kent
Printed and bound in Great Britain by
Chanctonbury Press Ltd, Bradford, West Yorkshire

Contents

DAVID WRIGHT

Foreword

There are many things to be said against the very idea of anthologies, those sticky bags of sweets where even the real toffee seems to lose its taste. As a clear statement of the case against them, *A Pamphlet Against Anthologies* by Robert Graves and Laura Riding (1928) remains unanswered and indeed unanswerable. All the same, fifty-seven years on, anthologies continue to be compiled and published, presumably to satisfy the needs of a public hungry for beauty and/or truth in small doses, and here I am apologizing for having made the present one. By way of excuse, I can only say that I think it might have been worse had the editor been X or Y, either of whom may always be relied upon to include more fashionable names, or simply more names altogether, in order to sell their products. My brief from P.E.N. was straightforward: to assemble in three months of early 1985 an anthology of mostly unpublished verse of which one third would be by 'known' poets and the rest by the little-known or unknown. To this end, P.E.N. kindly supplied me with 2441 pieces of stuff resembling verse, which they had obtained after advertising for it. I might claim that I read all of this diligently, though most of it fell into that category mentioned I think in the *Book of Common Prayer* of 'things we neither desire nor deserve'. Still, there *were* real poets and real poems to be found in that mountain of manuscripts, and I hope that the reader will recognize them where they appear here. For the rest, I solicited contributions from a number of poets, known, little-known, and even unknown (save to their peers), and was very grateful when most of them responded. The result is this anthology in which you will find 163 poems by fifty-four poets. That is fewer poets but rather more poems per poet than is perhaps usual in books of this kind, but then it has always been my belief that there are never as many poets in any age as there seem to be, and Time, the only critic worth his tools, will without doubt sort out the present lot far more severely than I have. Meanwhile, I can hope that you, the reader, will find here small but representative selections from the work of poets who may prove new to you, or if not new then previously unrecognized for their true worth, as well as work by famous poets which will seem to you not unworthy of their fame. In other words, I trust that there is enough real toffee, by real toffee-makers, to make the anthology both immediately palatable and possibly durable as an example of what there was to be collected and put into a bag of poetic 'sweets' by one man in the spring of 1985. Acknowledgements are due to Bernard Stone, The Many Press, the *Scotsman*, *PN Review*, the *TLS*, *Spectator*, *Agenda*, *London Magazine*, *New Statesman*, *Encounter* and the *New Yorker* where some of these poems will have appeared by the time this anthology is published.

R.N.

P.E.N.
New Poetry I

Dannie Abse

MILLIE'S DATE

With sedative voices we joke and spar
as white coats struggle around her bed.
Millie's IO2, all skull; once her head
was lovely – eyes serious, lips ready to be kissed
at Brixham, in 'the County of Heaven'.
She's outlived three wars and three husbands.
Her only child 'passed over', aged 77.

Sometimes she plucks the life-line in her small
left hand; remarks, 'An itch means money.'
Mostly, though, she's glum or incontinent
with memories. But now, like that immortal
at Cumae who hung in a jar, she cries,
'Let me die, let me die,' – silencing us.
How should we reply? With unfunny science?

Or, 'Not to worry – the Angels of Death
survive forever'? Often I've wondered
if some are disguised as vagrants, assigned
to each of us and programmed to arrive
punctually for their seedy appointments.
So where's Millie's escort, in which doss-house?
Has he lost his way, has he lost his mind?

Millie's quiet now, in a valium doze,
and window by window the building darkens
as lights go home. Outside, I half-expect
a doss-house beggar with a violin
to play, 'Ah, sweet mystery of Life' – some song
like that. Then any passer-by could drop
two coins, as big as eyes, inside his hat.

3

Not wishing to pronounce the taboo word
I used to write, 'Acid-fast organisms'.
Earlier physicians noted with a quill,
'The animalcules generate their own kind
and kill.' Some lied. Or murmured, 'Phthisis,
King's Evil, Consumption, Koch's Disease'.
But friend of student days, John Roberts, clowned,
'TB I've got. You know what TB signifies?
Totally buggered.' He laughed. His sister cried.
The music of sound is the sound of music.

And what of that other medical student,
that other John, coughing up redness on
a white sheet? 'Bring me the candle, Brown.
That is arterial blood, I cannot be deceived
in that colour. It is my death warrant.'
The cruelty of Diseases! This one, too.
For three centuries, in London, the slow, sad bell.
Helplessly, wide-eyed, one in five died of it.
Doctors prescribed, 'Horse-riding, Sir, ride and ride'.
Or diets, rest, mountain air, sea-voyages.

Today, an X-ray on this oblong light
clear that was not clear. No pneumothorax,
no deforming thoracoplasty. No flaw.
The patient nods, accepts it as his right
and is right. Later, alone, I, questing for
old case-histories, open the tight desk-drawer
to smell again Schiller's rotten apples.

A SCREAM

That scream from the street erased all content,
that uninspired cry of lunacy
left a vacuum. The ears of our cat

like clown-hats lifted. And silence extended
till this room, at midnight, resumed with one
manic bluebottle tap-tapping the lampshade.

Then you, brave, concerned, pulled the curtains back.
We saw only the emptiness of our street
in lamplight. No blind hunter stumbled by

four times the size of a man. So many
enigmas! That night I dreamt we opened
the little wooden boxes of spikenard,

frankincense, cinnamon, saffron and myrrh;
also that herb from which can rise the antique
S-shaped, slate-coloured smoke to Paradise.

Peter Ackroyd

AND THE CHILDREN. . .

and the children who see everything
forget: what is separate
is also in succession, the will empties
and is replaced by the shape
of moving things

as you were running beside me
and night comes on,
a room is a fragile place
in which to remember
and catch the warmth as it flies

second by second
to recreate what was not created,
making the figure still
as it was at first sight,
the half-light upon the floor

IT WOULD BE EASY. . .

it would be easy to get lost
in a prosaic description of this light
on water, clause upon clause
opening out into a description of light
praised for its subtlety and distance

talking in your sleep
is another way, the evidence of senses
left in bewilderment
at the sight of all there is
the soul creeping into the dark

each thing with its own wish to grow
and avert its face,
the penniless young man
smiles at the light
the nearest thing to oblivion

ALL THESE. . .

---

all these particles of knowledge
are a stick which I carry in my hand
pulled out of the vast emptiness
of a day at the sea

I looked up into the branches
and I saw nothing
except the wind
and its persistent insect

the dunes incline towards me
and the noisome truth
is the knowledge
that you will have to leave this place

the branch floating down
haunted by itself
as a body
having to change what it loves

THE DAY. . .

the day has been drawn off
into a shoulder of brown cloth

the vehicle waits
in which she sits, unencumbered

the child already
marked in that way

the pain comes in
the song of the tin man

and the song has gone
I think this is what Eliot meant
except that I don't think

the words are short
in the mouth, tranquillity
is not one of them

John Ash

THE HOTEL BROWN POEMS

1. Above every seaward-facing window
   of the Hotel Brown is a canopy. At night
   the perfumes of the garden will delight you. . .

   It is a good place to fall in love
   and a good place to write, though neither
   is obligatory. You must, however,

   praise the light, the changing colours
   of the sea at dawn and dusk: these are
   the divinities of the place. Amen.

2. Once in the cool, blue restaurant
   of the Hotel Brown a friend said to me, –
   'You don't realise how much your openness
   frightens people: it hits them like a wave,'

   and I smiled, not because his words
   amused me, but because the scent of peppers
   grilling in the kitchen overwhelmed me.
   I could not think of ideas or people then –

   only of the place, the scent, the way
   long white curtains moved back and forth
   across the boundaries of light and air.

3. The windows were open on to the small terrace.
   The sea was motionless. Not a wave. I would not,
   for the world, compare it to anything.

I pointed down the half-deserted quay
drowsy with a heat that seemed personal
like a memory, and said 'That man, hunched

as if he were struggling against
a cold wind, is a poet, a friend of mine.
Let's make ourselves known.'

4. Think of yourself as a wave. Hard.
   Think of yourself as open. Equally hard.
   Usually your gestures seem to take place
   behind a glass partition, fogged with steam

   and there is often the sense that things are closing in, –
   have closed over you like the waters of a lamentation,
   and the absence of obvious locks or bars only confirms
   that, depressingly, the fault lies in your soul as much

   as hostile circumstances, the invisible clouds
   of general despondency that hang off even the most
   blissful shore, waiting to blow in, dulling
   the water, the boats, your deepest words with dust.

5. As we walked towards the temple
   the poet said to us: 'This may seem
   a small island to you but once it was
   an independent state with its own fierce navy.

   The Athenians destroyed it utterly.'
   The old ramparts were massive, finely jointed
   but the area of jumbled stones and bushes they enclosed
   seemed no bigger than a modest public park.

6. We saw him to the evening boat. A man
   who walked like a dancer followed him aboard
   carrying a single bicycle wheel, and the ship
   departed, illuminated, unreasonably festive.

   We walked back past the bars. The night
   was already richly dark, full of murmured conversation.

10

Light poured down the steps of the Hotel Brown,
traversed by a cold, rising breeze, as if to say –

'You are welcome, for the moment. This
is an interval in your life. Soon you must look to
the plots and masks and backdrops of your next act.
Here all moments are intervals. It is like music and like
loss.'

MEMORIES OF ITALY (BROKEN SESTINA)

for Pat Steir

I loved the light of course
and the way the young men
flirted with each other.
I loved the light, –

the way it fell out of a sky like a painting,
or perhaps like the ground (if this
is not too paradoxical a way of
putting it) for a painting,

and the way the young men stood in the station
wearing jeans that were the colour of the sky
or the sea in a painting, jeans that revealed
the shapes of their legs which reminded me

of the statues in the square outside the station
where the light fell with such violence
their shadows were blacker than the despair of the painter
who cannot proceed with the painting: the canvas
is before him, its ground blue and black as the sky above the
station

where the young men loiter like heroes in one of the lulls of
the Trojan War
when lazy picnics were possible beside the calm sea, under
the smiling sky,

11

and it half seems that the war will end forever, for surely
they must all soon fall in love with each other. . .
And the painter knows his painting must be heroic, that the
blue is not the sky
but a terrible sea a God has raised to drown the beauty of the
young men in the marble battlefield of the station,

and he knows the painting is finished,
that it represents the envy the divine must feel
towards the human as marble must envy the sea,

and the painting is hung in the concourse of the station
and the young men drift indifferently to and fro before it:
their feet hardly seem to touch the blue marble ground.

EPIGRAPHS FOR EPIGONES

An inrush of children
turned the upper decks into an aviary.
From that vantage
we could see orange and mauve sweetpeas
obscuring the weathered sections of a fence.
There was hideous singing
and violent assertion of character
in the courteous face of death
who descended the stairs, not wishing
to cause embarrassment now or hereafter.
The rails were smudged with dust, and also
the several petals of the suburb
wilting like gloves
in the average torpor, in the muffled shrillness
that spoke of the need to choose
another scene.

The old violin case. The head of hair.
Crushed fruit. The faces drawn on paving stones.
A deer park or sailing boat. Letters
in the rainswept journal telling

of the ridiculous passions that convince,
are all that convinces . . . All these could be part of it
as long as they have the backing of a breeze
just starting up, gently, but fresh, indisputable
as dying or the pathos of evening traffic passing
below the city towers with a sound like catarrh:
all will be included in the new proposals
that really will be pasted up on the walls and the arches
someday soon, believe me! For now

the trivial journey with the shopping bags and children,
along canal banks crowded with the hope of salvation
(which appears as faded, nameless flowers) must continue, –

but think only of departure,
the clouds you will be lost in
and let your irresolution be a law.

Observe how the tired objects of the day,
living like trees, seem to shift with their desire
to be ornamental in their final moment.

THE OTHER GREAT COMPOSERS

They lived in places tourists don't care to visit
beside streams the obscure workings of local pride
insisted were rivers: there were willows or derelict mills
sometimes a boathouse with Palladian ambitions, –
in the backwoods, except that the towering pines were,
often as not, replaced by clusters of factory chimneys, –
isolate, the factories gone, the chimneys octagonal,
grand as columns remembering a Trajan victory
although severely unadorned. They lived in places where
commerce destroyed the Roman forts, the common fields
with red viaducts, canals now, like them, disused
and forgotten, depositories for ignorance or else
they sank into the confines of a half-suburban dream
or pastoral they couldn't share: the works grew longer,

'unperformable' . . . The aggression of the ordinary,
the tepid love expressed in summerhouses too small
really to contain lover and beloved, the muted modes
and folksongs rediscovered, dead as elms, drove them
to new forms of learning and excess, ruthless
distortions of the academic tones and tomes,
chords that decayed over log bars into distances
where bell-hung, bird-haunted pagodas of their own
design rose up, tier on tier, to radiant mountains, –
mountains from which they confidently expected,
year after year, the arrival of the ancient and youthful
messenger who would confirm the truth of these visions.
It is impossible yet to say that they were wrong:
the music is unproved and undisproved; their operas
require cathedrals in which the angels and grotesques
come alive for one scene only; their fugues and toccatas
demand the emergence of a pianist eight-handed
like a Hindu god whose temples remain a sheaf of sketches,
whose religion is confined to a single head, maddened
or happy, dead-centred in a continent of neglect.

THE WONDERFUL TANGERINES

1. Taking one's head off
   is an odd way of showing
   appreciation of the symphony,
   but this is what she has done, –
   the woman with the pastoral,
   Marie Antoinette air
   holding her smiling head
   on a level with her hips,
   and the guests murmur: 'Charming.
   So clever. I suppose it is done
   with mirrors'. But of course
   it isn't. Strange to look
   down on one's hat while
   it is still on one's head.
   The symphony is one of those

14

with picturesque titles, you know, –
The Claw-Hammer, The Flight-Bag,
The Spaniel, and so on . . .

2. 'My dear I must tell you
   about the cutlery.
   None of it would match
   and believing that music,
   in propitious circumstances,
   can alter the shape of
   material objects, he placed it
   in a transparent plastic
   container next to the piano.
   The concerto was a wild success
   but still the supper was a shambles.'

3. For the rhapsodies
   we arranged the grapes
   in violin cases
   under the German busts.

   The members of the quartet concealed themselves
   behind black curtains, only their hands
   protruding through the narrow apertures provided.
   The string emerged slowly from their cuffs.

   They began with a lyrical andante
   (composed by the principal string-master)
   – slender, variously tinted threads
   gently attenuated amid the eight, gesturing
   hands. The effect was most poignant,
   and they ended with the awesome counterpoint
   of a Grosse Fugue, a mesh
   so dense it might be mistaken
   for topiary. When a volunteer
   finally mounted the platform
   to pull a single, trailing strand
   and the entire, immense structure
   collapsed before our eyes
   the applause was tumultuous.

4. It is November.
   Cloud-shadows scud across
   the shallow lake water,
   and the Duke moves sadly
   towards the bathing huts.
   It is too late in the season to swim
   but this is not his intention.
   He approaches a pale, once royal-blue,
   much-weathered bathing hut
   and enters. He kneels down
   at the centre of the little room
   and raises his eyes towards the far wall.
   Nailed to it are six complete
   and luxurious sets of women's lingerie,
   a honeyed beige in colour.
   There is a space on the right
   for a seventh set. He reaches
   in his pocket and brings out
   the long, gleaming nails. A tear
   forms in his eye.

John Ashbery

BY THE FLOODED CANAL

Which custard? The dish of not-so-clean snow
Or the sherry trifle with bloodlike jam and riotous
Yellow stuff running down the steep sides
Into ambiguity, an ambiguous thing. Do you want me
To come here anymore.

Then I met your father.
I hadn't written anything for almost a year.

Unfortunately he wasn't very attractive.

He married a woman with the curious name of Lael.
It all took me by surprise, coming up behind me
Like a book. As I stand and look at it now.
Then all the thoughts went out of my head,
Running away into the wind. I didn't have *him*
To think about anymore, I didn't have myself either.
It was all notes for a book, or footnotes, footnotes
For a book that has been written, that nobody
Is ever going to read. A bottle with a note in it
Washes up on shore and no one sees it, no one picks it up.

And then one day it was windy
With fog, and I hate the combination of fog and wind,
Besides being too cool for what it looked like. The sun
Was probably out just a short distance above our heads.
Not a good drying day. And I hung the laundry out
On the clothes-line, all black and white
And the news got lost somewhere inside. My news.

Do you come here any longer with the intention of killing

Something, no you have nothing in mind.
And I shift, arranging the pieces
In a cardboard drawer. No two are alike, and I like that.

The kitten on the stairs heard it
Once, in disbelief, and I go
To sales, and buy only what we need.
The old men are a strong team.

And I mix it up with them, it's quite like
Having encounters if one is a poplar
In a row of them and so involved
With one's reflection as well as one's two neighbours only I
say
I didn't mean for it to be this way
But since it has happened I'm glad and will continue to
work,
To strive for your success. I don't expect thanks
And am happy in the small role assigned me,
Really. I think I'll go out in the garage.

WET ARE THE BOARDS

Not liking what life has in it,
'It's probably dead, whatever it is,'
You said, and turned, and thought
Of one spot on the ground, what it means to all of us
Passing through the earth. And the filleted, reasonable
Nymph of the fashions of the air points to that too:
'No need to be deprived. We are all
Friends here,
And whatever it takes to get us out of the mess we're in,
One of us has.'

Charming, you thought. The spirited bulk,
The work of a local architect, knows how to detach itself
From the little puffs issuing from the mouths of the four
winds,

Yet not too much, and be honest
While still remaining noble and sedate.
The tepees on the front lawn
Of the governor's palace became a fixture there
And were cast in stone when the originals rotted away.
Fish tanks glinted from within the varnished
Halls of jurisprudence and it was possible to save
The friezes, of Merovingian thrust,
And so much else made to please the senses
Like a plum tree dripping besmirched brilliants
On a round dirt bed, and all the stories of the ducks.
Now if only I were a noncombatant –
Which brings us back to the others: philosophers,
Pedants, and criminals intent on enjoying the public view –
Is it just another panorama

In my collection, or do I belong to it
As long as it wishes to regard me? For we none of us
Can determine strictly what they are thinking,
Even the one we walk arm in arm with
Through the darkling purple air of spring, so when it comes
Time to depart our goodbyes will read automatically true or
false
According to what has gone before.
And that loneliness will accompany us
On the far side of parting, when what we dream, we read.
No hand is outstretched
Through the bored gloom unless more thinking wants to
take us elsewhere
Into a space that seems changed, by luck or just by time
hanging around,
And the mystery of the family that bore you
Into the race that is.

And get involved in it we did, reversing the story
So that the end showed through the paper as the beginning
And all children were nice again.
Think again of the scenery
Whirling to destroy itself, and what a different face
It wears when order smiles, as I know it
Does here. The costumes we wore
Must never be folded and put back into the trunk again,
Or someone too young for the part is going to step up

And say, 'Listen, I made it. It's mine,'
In a November twilight when the frost is creeping over you
As surely as waves across a beach, since no chill is complete
Without your unique participation. And when you walk away
    away
You might reflect that this is an aspect
In which all of the cores and seeds are visible.
It's a matter of not choosing to see.

Elizabeth Baines

NEWS OF OLD GIRLS

High School Magazine, Autumn 1964

Heartiest congratulations to Emma Slade this autumn.
She is going on: our ex-head-girl graduates from London
to further the frontiers of Science at Durham
studying the diseases of chrysanthemums.

Fresh from Reading with a second in Languages
is Amanda Brown. She ventures into both teaching and
      marriage.
'The true Nigerians are charming,' writes Elsie Savage,
an adventurous soul, now leaving Voluntary Service.

Phyllis Hall has been discovered on the staff of Bell's
      Academy;
Domestic Science. She and her girls dispensed tea that was
      excellent.
Fiona Callan is making good use of artistic talents:
assistant buyer, Harrods' gift selection.

Janet Sugden has a niche at Barrowmore's optician's,
downtown. She keeps the waiting-room lively with flowers.
Back from London (she does not report why), Susan Briggs
takes the SCHEME FOR YOUNG LADIES at British
      Wires.

To those who have taken abroad the Spirit of School
all credit – not forgetting Arleen Ash, radiography cram
– *no hint of Anne James, found smoking, expelled,*
unrecognised afterwards pushing her pram –

or Olga Sedge in charge of ropes in the kitchens at Durham,
alongside our far-reaching Emma – *passed on,*
breast cancer, 1970, autumn.
The school sent chrysanthemums.

George Barker

THE IKONS OF THE DEAD

to Edward

I
But was there time? No,
    there was never time.
There was only the breath
exhaled by the first burning
babe from a cloud, lasting
the whole of one flaming moment
before the ashes fell.

II
Where was the place? The place
    was not here.
Some far where else the
    celebration of bells,
    the house of sacred things,
the rider on the bull, the dying
    serpent's tears,
    the peacock crying
and, like knives in the sky,
    extraordinary wings.

III
Can I come back to you?
    No one is there.
They are all gone. No one was
    ever there.
The mask of the holy man has
    faded now and
the silence is not golden.

Through love shall we
labour to give birth to
    death, when the fiery
mountain and the inverted
    dog inherit the earth.

IV
Who was there? No one was
    ever there, where
the hands meet at midnight and
    the wave, breaking,
hangs for ever over
    rocks that cannot speak. There
you will find a face staring
    out of eyes
that cannot see the sea.

V
The leopard may sleep in chains
    and the nebula
bare a sunburst in its
    breast but
no dreams attend those cold
    lairs, no bone
grows from the grave there,
but, sleeping, the gleam of the phoenix
    in the spread of its sunburst
dreams of old bones.

VI
And over October fields a single
    death stalks out of its life into
a river of subterranean springs.
    Haunted by knowledge it walks
into the lunar and erotic cave.
    And then the scarecrow speaks
of love to a ghost in the laurel grove.

VII
Whose blood drips from the engines? Whose?
    Overhead I hear the crack of
    February glass and the lightning
    dance in November coffins.

Five loves
multiply zeroes and crosses in the air
and where I seek you, find
wounds only, wounds with wings,
     wounds like knives.

VIII

Who are those apes sedulously
     re-setting type
that no one can ever read? Apples
     appear at the tips
of the god's fingers
     then deflate like bladders
because we know
     Laiki has always murdered
golden Apollo. These
     the images of eternal impermanence.

IX

Whose was the voice? From
     far off effigies
I hear the lyrics of
     those Grecian liars who
died for information.
     Will the table rise flapping
like an open book in the air
     and the alphabet, in a dance,
in a trance, continually declare
     the word is love, but there
is no word there.

X

Later the moon, rising over Russia
drew pyramidical constructions
     of white skulls out of
the steppes of the past, until I thought
I gazed upon philosophical battlements
dividing Europe and the hordes of bones
battling behind my eyes. Then
among those fallen I came upon my star.

XI

The lesser mysteries always contain the greater

just as the zero multiplies or the circle
retreats into the recurring seven to leave us
wandering along a seashore where Isaac Newton
      contemplating coloured pebbles
takes by the arm a winged Victory that whispers:
      Every one is everyone today.

XII

I have not learned the ceremonies of salvation
if they are not like this. They go,
the young dog dancing after old Adam,
and the flayed babe singing,
and Aphrodite, her belly full of cupids,
alighting tiptoe on rocks,
all ceaselessly chanting in flames, ceaselessly chanting.

Alan Bold

DAVID HUME, DYING, TALKS TO BOSWELL

---

7 July 1776

Sunday, Boswell, and you visit *me*:
Too late for church this Sunday?
I'm back now, as you see,
From Bath and London . . . but you frown
At my appearance. Come, stay
Near a dying man and sit down.

I still reckon on a speedy dissolution
From that disorder in my bowels. Sick
In body, my mind's in motion.
I'm approaching my end, Boswell.
Now Dr Campbell's *Philosophy of Rhetorick*
Can wait and we can talk a while.

The morality of every religion is bad, Boswell.
When I hear a man is
Religious I conclude he is a rascal.
Immortality would put the sage
Beside the rabble – in new universes
Built to take the trash of every age.

As for annihilation, Boswell, the thought
Of it's no different from the idea
Of never having been, to cite
Lucretius and, dear Boswell,
A future state would not necessarily be a
Heaven. There's always a Phlegethon or Hell.

From their actions in this world are men
And their abilities judged. I grow fonder
Of the Stuart family and perhaps my pen
Has vindicated the first two.
No need, dear Boswell, to wonder:
I have no pain but am wasting away.

CONCERNING CORK

On the water, cork floats
Beside the buoyant fishing boats.
What can one say about cork?
Linguistically it chimes with work
But the uncorked bottle suggests
This is misleading: drinking with guests
Is hardly business (though some
Businessmen make such a claim).
Proust enjoyed his cork-lined room
In which he reconstructed time.
Cork, capital-lettered, becomes
Cork, in Eire, which James
Joyce valued in his father's name:
In Paris, in a real cork frame,
He kept a photo of the place.
Cork, of course, protects trees
And shrubs; the cork-oak
Produces the commercial cork
Which helps control the tone
On my alto-saxophone
(As, smeared with cork-grease,
It slides into the mouthpiece).
That's cork, supple to the touch;
Not, normally, valued overmuch.
It is invaded through and through;
The turn of the corkscrew.

Among the offwhite walls where flowers
Suffocate with fragile smiles
It's the shock that stuns, the sneak blow
Delivered in deadly earnest,
That stamps the matter of fact over the illusion.
Tonight I heard my mother was dying
Yet there she was, warm in the ward,
Her skin healthy and her face flushed
With the unexpected excitement of it all:
The deliberations with doctors,
The confidential chats with consultants,
The whole holy hierarchy of hospital.
She had never seemed so important
In a life spent scrubbing stairs,
Serving in shops, and babyminding rich adults.
I was summoned by a doctor,
A trim young woman looking drawn,
And thought I was ready for anything.
Still, I didn't see the sneak blow coming,
For all that she prepared me:
'I'm afraid,' she said, 'it's bad news.'
The rest was vague
As she spelled out the symptoms,
Delivered the death sentence.
The news seeped in slowly
As I returned to my mother
And saw her, clearly, dying
With the cancer curled inside her.
She had a limit on her life,
A matter of months.
There was nothing more to say
But words that hung
Enormous in the antiseptic air.
I left with my daughter and my wife,
The two remaining women in my life.

THE PUBLIC WASH HOUSE

for Ken Duffy

Something of a sauna for working women,
Or home from home for housewives,
The steamie had them all in hot water
As the warmth rose onto white-tiled walls.
Dear women, they swarmed there
With nappies, shirts and sheets
And took the plunge
While the kids hung around in the crèche upstairs.
They were glad to succumb to the clatter.
The clothes horses, the hot air,
The odour of Turkish baths,
The gurgling of gossip.
Trailing their children they took pramfuls of washing,
Trundled down the Wash House Brae,
Having done what they had to do.
They went home, steam still in their nostrils,
Their hands rubbed raw, scrubbed red;
But with their washing done
Their world was larger, being clean,
And the children seemed to shine.

THE CELTIC ALBATROSS

The wandering albatross rides the wind,
Scaring sailors with storms,
Drinking saltwater and scorning the land
Until it is time to breed.
But the Celtic albatross
Claims a victim
Who walks under the weight of it,
Caught in its clutches,
Carrying it reluctantly,
A cause, a cross, a corpse.

So you try to escape.
You sense, in the distance,
A great globe of light,
Tawny and blue and white:
Contours of continents,
Azures of the atmosphere,
Coverings of clouds.
And the clouds,
They are weeping rain
Upon the earth.
The albatross descends.

Now you are in the dark,
A Celtic creature,
An adjunct of the albatross.
You want to look up
For there is this one light,
This round circle of light.

When you reach out to touch
It is light years out of your reach.

D. Brennan

TOAD SONG

Let's hear it for the toads,
hopping along the road
supporting the geniuses.

I am the toad that provides you with your daily bread
and I'm sick of your condescension
that you pour on my not-so-toad head.

Who reads, listens, croaks your name?
Pays your wages, builds your fame?
Toads are your total audience.

I am the toad that provides you with your bread and butter
and I'm sick of your condescension
which is all that your genius tongue is able to utter.

A genius behind a green plastic mask
doing your share of despised toad tasks.
That's how you're able to be so bright.

I am the toad that provides you with your bread and jam
and I'm sick of your condescension
that unseeingly tolerates all (you suppose) that I am.

Stanley Cook

The thought that in a single day,
Especially by getting up an hour
Earlier, you could put,
If not the world, at least your life
Completely in order, blunts itself
By half-past nine. I sit in the car
Opposite the doctor's opposite the park
And nothing, again, has taken an edge.
The bowling green is spread but empty
And the closed recreation hut
In the shadow of the trees
Full of a green aquarium gloom.
Cloud snags on the tops
Of distant public buildings or overhead
Spits rain. Prams, dogs
And regulars at the morning surgery
Who demonstrate most of all
Life, in some ways, is incurable
Go by. A boy in a monster mask,
At the wrong time to frighten anyone,
Goes unexcitedly into the park.

THE BLIND UPHOLSTERER

The blind upholsterer whose handicap
Equips him, in lieu of other gifts,
To professional standard, allowing him
To feel the shape within the dark
As a sculptor feels it within the stone,
Knew the blindness was in the family
He wasn't surprised to be overtaken by.
He always kept a dog in any case
And the barman and tobacconist
Knew his order without his having to ask.
This, though, he wouldn't have done
Half so well while still he saw,
Having now no choice but to succeed.
I who shut my eyes in a final effort
To turn a key or untie a knot
Can only imagine how much he sheds
That stands in the way of the feel of a needle.

SHEFFIELD EAST END

Usually a landscape more obviously beautiful
Moves through our lives – rocks and running water
Measuring us down to decimals of grass,
The grasshoppers in it and butterflies
And flower petals unpicking in even smaller
Units of time. Buildings mark off an era
By changes of style. What – now it is gone –
They call the working-class heartland
But demolished under the name of slums
Is fields again the second time round
That last was fields two centuries ago.
Unused roads, not hedges, divide the green

Blocked in roughly with tall coarse plants
Literally sometimes far as the eye can see.
The logic that levelled hundreds of houses here,
Whose rehoused tenants still come back for the shops,
Has blown away. The classic sign of recession –
Grass growing where wheels once trod it out –
Has made its point but keeps on growing and growing.
Such a shock that this can really happen
To cities whose lives stretched parallel with ours.
A window high in a solitary works
Is utterly empty (or full, if you like, of sky)
Where the opposite wall has already gone.
It isn't just grass that's growing,
But flowers supposedly rare inland in the North
That, crushed, release scents new to me.

CALDER VALLEY: AT THE TOP OF THE AINLEYS

Concrete somersaults cleanly in a bridge
Over the lorries coming up in the crawler lane;
The road no longer falls, twisting and turning,
Off the site of the hill, but a by-pass
Shoots a hole and swoops on the valley.
Through the hole the panorama
Of the farther side surprises you,
Moorland the nineteenth century burdened
With mills foursquare and houses back to back,
And from this height, before the by-pass glides
To a level landing a mile away,
The hole is a peephole, much as a single life
Must once have been on an age:
You see it all and have to become a part.

'Sixty-seven years ago on Sunday,' he said,
Supporting himself against the tubular scaffolding
Outside old offices being steamwashed,
'On my eighteenth birthday, I landed at Gallipoli.
No, I've not been well: fell down three times
And they tell me I shouldn't drive.' His bright eyes
    brightened
And his flushed cheeks flushed, caught as he was
Between the pills that pepped him up and the pills
That slowed him down. Abruptly he clapped a hand
Down on my shoulder, whether for emphasis
Or further support, it was hard to tell.
'Look after yourself,' he said.

Neil Curry

MEMORIAL TO THE VICARS OF URSWICK

for Brian Dawson

I don't know if Matthias Forrest
Would have been taken greatly by surprise
When the news broke in Furness that his parishioners
Had sprung from apes. 'Liars, drunkards, thieves,
And whoremasters following their filthy pleasures',
That was how George Fox had seen them;
And one of his own brothers in Christ had been disgraced:
'Scandalous in his life and negligent in his calling.'

Fragments of the parish history
Survive to flesh out the names on the plaque
That Thomas Postlethwaite had put up in the chancel;
Telling us that one February
John Addison roasted a whole ox on the ice
When the Tarn had frozen over;
And that it was William Ashburner who arranged
And officiated at the cock-fights on Shrove Tuesday.

Great events of course can be worked out
From the dates: that the first awful reading
From the King James Bible would have been William
    Lindowe's,
And that it was Nicholas Marshall
Who walked in with the Book of Common Prayer, and then
Had to hold out against Cromwell.
And back, through the collapse of the monastery,
Their names go, till that last, first one, Daniel le Fleming,

Who'd have needed a smooth Norman tongue
To lick the North into holy order.
But the wonder of it all is how few of them
There were. Call them together again
And what a flimsy congregation they would seem:
Three pews would seat them all. And yet,
With time spread out like these low fells, one name's no
    more
Than that sudden twist in the tumbling flight of a plover.

GARDENS

We smiled together
over the precepts in that old herbal,
vowing, as we valued our eyesight,
never to gather
the fruit of the peony
save at dead of night
and thus 'all unseene of the woodpecker',

noted too that powdered
periwinkle and earthworm, if taken
at mealtimes, does rekindle a wife's
love for her husband;
strange that they would tolerate
such wild beliefs
in days when heretics, not weeds, got burned.

But what gardeners they were:
what arbours of trellis work; embroidered
intricacies of bright nosegay-knots;
thrift and lavender-
scented walks of evergreen;
what salves and syrops
of simple herbs for health and provender;

what workers for Eden.
Though few of us today would freely voice

38

our dreams of unicorns and rosebuds,
their secret garden
has alleyways that may yet
outpace all our thoughts.
What our lives lack is what our hands fashion.

The Moghul emperor,
Babur, blazed and butchered his way across
the steppes of Asia, then called a halt
while his warriors
erected walls around one
cool sequestered spot
where lilacs shaded white shawls of water.

THE MAIDENHAIR TREE

It was a tree that neither of us
had ever seen before,
its trunk lined and grey, its leaves
like little pairs of green webbed feet
and strangely fleshy,

but what really stopped us as we stepped
from stained-glass cloistered gloom
into impartial sunlight?
Remembering Thoreau saying
how monstrous he thought

it was that people cared so little
about trees, yet so much
for Corinthian columns?
Or the affront of namelessness,
the one challenge still

capable of overwhelming knowledge
in that its secret lies
not in saying but being:
and not the tawdry masquerades
of reverie, the

fictions and frippery of longing,
　　　but plainly and truly
what for the beholder *is*:
the embodiment of the one
　　　moment; for language

however deftly it may be used
　　　in the flora, will not
explain the susurrations
of dry leaves, and illustration,
　　　though perfect of line,

shows nothing of the rings' slow stretching
　　　and splitting, the great thirst
sucking moisture from the black
earth to breathe it out through the green
　　　veins of its foliage;

but such realities always must
　　　admit experience,
not just the thing perceived but
the experience likewise of
　　　the perceiving mind,

so that tree now cannot simply be
　　　without the cathedral
close we first found it in, and
our shared memories, both of which
　　　lie beyond telling.

JOHN CLARE AND THE ACTS OF ENCLOSURE

Emmonsales Heath was the last rim of the world.
A child could see that. Once there he would kneel
And peer down over the dreadful edge of it
And learn its secrets. Just one good day's walk
Was all it needed. But night, closing in,
Found his feet tired and turning for home.

Next it was the Enclosures Man who baulked him,
Fencing the land with lines of quickthorn
And leaving him only the plod of words
To get there – words that Taylor would root up
And level out, planting crops of commas
That tore like thistles through his thoughts.

So hedged about, where else was there to go?
Safer indoors perhaps with Dr Prichard. . .
He never could have guessed they meant to chop
Off his head and steal away his alphabet,
All those pretty vowels and consonants,
Tweezering them out, one by one, through his ears.

Gloria Evans Davies

BANQUET

The parrot teased
            With fan after fan
        Looks with a wary eye
            At the moon,
The old Emperor
    Preferring to be
            With the cherry trees,
                His favourite daughter
Out of favour
    For unbinding her feet
                Bound tighter,
The Empress's eyebrows
            In a new green
Of the green-spotted mushroom;
        Beneath
                His unsuspecting gaze
Over the wine-spilt
                Chrysanthemums,
                    Plums
Her lover had thrown
            To her
From terraces of jade –
                Their horses nibbling
            The grass coat
                Of a water-carrier
On the wall of a well.
                Willow plaits willow,
His daughter wishing
    She could lean against
                Her paper window
To ease her pain,

Between showers
Peacocks scream
As if their feet
Are bound like hers;
A banished drunk
On a small balcony
Shares a sleeping mat
With an overhanging apricot branch,
Swallows
Wheel into the courtyard
As tightly
As around a chimney;
Small children
Of the palace
Put her embroidered shells
To their ears.

Dick Davis

IBN BATTUTA

Near the beginning of his first journey
The great traveller – who was to suffer
Shipwreck, the loss of all his wealth, his slaves
(On whom he doted) and his son; who was
To fight with pirates, brigands, be received
By princes as an equal and be laughed at
As a pauper; who was to see the known world
And its wonders – near the beginning
Of his first journey he tells us how
In company with a caravan of travellers
He approached a city, and how a crowd
Of well-wishers and relatives came out
To welcome them, so that each man was greeted
By a face he knew, except for him,
Ibn Battuta, whom no one greeted
Because he was a stranger there, and how
This knowledge was borne in on him, and how
He wept.   When the book is closed, this picture
Of the young man in his twenties weeping
– And not the princes, slaves and shipwrecks –
Is what stays with you, so that you almost feel
Across the centuries the pressure of
Your hand against his arm, and hear
Your own voice raised in greeting.

CHEBUTYKIN

in Chekhov's Three Sisters

If I drop the clock it shatters –
Can I swear that this is true?
Never mind though, nothing matters.

Somewhere, someone vainly chatters
– How to live and what to do –
If I drop the clock it shatters.

No one listens: madam natters
– Dresses, servants, babies, 'flu –
Never mind though, nothing matters.

A household crazy as hatters;
But no . . . I haven't a clue.
If I drop the clock it shatters.

I suppose my life's in tatters . . .
To be honest that's not new.
Never mind though, nothing matters.

Kindness comforts us and flatters –
Nothing else will see us through.
If I drop the clock it shatters.
Never mind though, nothing matters.

Cozette de Charmoy

FROM DELPHI

Here I am again
so what's new
I ask you
Here to prepare for
the long boring day ahead
First the ritual wash
Purification if you prefer
next fumigation
laurel leaves and barley meal
Now to chew the leaves
and wait
It's a bad smell in here all right
I'll be looped
sitting on this tripod all day
and me until recently
a respectable woman
old enough to know better
Why they have to choose a peasant
I don't know
The god prefers it they say
It's safer
no risk of rape
who'd rape an old peasant woman
like you they say
I don't know about that
We live in a strange world
things aren't what they were
anything can happen today
and often does
I've read the statistics
But I don't complain
it's just another job
that's the way I see it
if you see what I mean

Carol Ann Duffy

DEAR NORMAN

I have turned the newspaper boy into a diver
for pearls. I can do this. In my night
there is no moon, and if it happens that I speak
of stars it's by mistake. Or if it happens
that I mention these things it is by design.

His body is brown, breaking through waves. Such white
   teeth.
Beneath the water he searches for the perfect shell.
He does not know that, as he posts the *Mirror*
through the door, he is equal with dolphins.
I shall name him Pablo, because I can.

Pablo laughs and shakes the seaweed from his hair.
Translucent on his palm a pearl appears. He is reminded.
Cuerpo de mujer, blancas colinas, muslos blancos.
I find this difficult, and then again easy,
as I watch him push his bike off in the rain.

As I watch him push his bike off in the rain
I trace his name upon the window-pane.
There is little to communicate, but I have re-arranged
the order of the words. Pablo say You want for me
to dive again? I want for you to dive.

Tomorrow I shall deal with the dustman.

47

Tutumantu is like hopscotch, kwani-kwani is like hide-and-
    seek.
When my sister came back to Africa she could only speak
English. Sometimes we fought in bed because she didn't
    know
what I was saying. I like Africa better than England.
My mother says You will like it when we get our own house.
We talk a lot about the things we used to do
in Africa and then we are happy.

Wayne. Fourteen. Games are for kids. I support
the National Front. Paki-bashing and pulling girls'
knickers down. Dad's got his own mini-cab. We watch
the video. I Spit on Your Grave. Brilliant.
I don't suppose I'll get a job. It's all them
coming over here to work. Arsenal.

Masjid at 6 o'clock. School at 8. There was
a friendly shop selling rice. They ground it at home
to make chapattis. Baarrh is a small red fruit.
There was much more room to play than here in London.
We played in an old village. It is empty now.
We got a plane to Heathrow. People wrote to us
that everything was easy here.

It's boring. Get engaged. Probably work in Safeways
worst luck. I haven't lost it yet because I want
respect. Marlon Frederic's nice but he's a bit dark.
I like Madness. The lead singer's dead good.
My mum is bad with her nerves. She won't
let me do nothing. Tracey. It's just boring.

Ejaz. They put some sausages on my plate.
As I was going to put one in my mouth
a Moslem boy jumped on me and pulled.
The plate dropped on the floor and broke. He asked me in
    Urdu

if I was a Moslem. I said Yes. You shouldn't be eating this.
It's a pig's meat. So we became friends.

My sister went out with one. There was murder.
I'd like to be mates, but they're different from us.
Some of them wear turbans in class. You can't help
taking the piss. I'm going in the Army.
No choice really. When I get married
I might emigrate. A girl who can cook
with long legs. Australia sounds all right.

Some of my family are named after the Moghul emperors.
Aurangzeb, Jehangir, Batur, Humayun. I was born
thirteen years ago in Jhelum. This is a hard school.
A man came in with a milk crate. The teacher told us
to drink our milk. I didn't understand what she was saying,
so I didn't go to get any milk. I have hope and am ambitious.
At first I felt as if I was dreaming, but I wasn't.
Everything I saw was true.

ALPHABET FOR AUDEN

When the words have gone away
there is nothing left to say.

Unformed thought can never be,
what you feel is what you see,
write it down and set it free
on printed pages, © Me.
I love, you love, so does he –
long live English Poetry.
Four o'clock is time for tea,
I'll be Mother, who'll be me?

Murmur, underneath your breath,
incantations to the deaf.

Here we go again. Goody.
Art can't alter History.

49

Praise the language, treasure each
well-earned phrase your labours reach.

In hotels you sit and sigh,
crafting lines where others cry,

puzzled why it doesn't pay
shoving couplets round all day.
There is vodka on a tray.
Up your nose the hairs are grey.

When the words done gone it's hell
having nothing left to tell.

Pummel, punch, fondle, knead them
back again to life. Read them

when you doubt yourself and when
you doubt their function, read again.

Verse can say *I told you so*
but cannot sway the status quo

one inch. Now you get lonely,
Baby want love and love only.

In the mirror you see you.
Love you always, darling. True.

When the words have wandered far
poets patronise the Bar,

understanding less and less
Truth is anybody's guess

and Time's a clock, five off three,
mix another G & T.

Set 'em up, Joe, make that two.
Wallace Stevens thought in blue.

Words drown in a drunken sea,
dumb, they clutch at memory.

Pissed you have a double view,
something else to trouble you.

Inspiration clears the decks –
if all else fails, write of sex.

Every other word's a lie,
ain't no rainbow in the sky.

Some get lucky, die in bed,
one word stubbed in the ashtray. *Dead*.

THE DOLPHINS

World is what you swim in, or dance, it is simple.
We are in our element but we are not free.
Outside this world you cannot breathe for long.
The other has my shape. The other's movement
forms my thoughts. And also mine. There is a man
and there are hoops. There is a constant flowing guilt.

We have found no truth in these waters,
no explanations tremble on our flesh.
We were blessed and now we are not blessed.
After travelling such space for days we began
to translate. It was the same space. It is
the same space always and above it is the man.

And now we are no longer blessed, for the world
will not deepen to dream in. The other knows
and out of love reflects me for myself.
We see our silver skin flash by like memory
of somewhere else. There is a coloured ball
we have to balance till the man has disappeared.

The moon has disappeared. We circle wellworn grooves
of water on a single note. Music of loss forever
from the other's heart which turns my own to stone.

There is a plastic toy. There is no hope. We sink
to the limits of this pool until the whistle blows.
There is a man and our mind knows we will die here.

LIZZIE, SIX

What are you doing?
I'm watching the moon.
I'll give you the moon
when I get up there.

Where are you going?
To play in the fields.
I'll give you fields,
bend over that chair.

What are you thinking?
I'm thinking of love.
I'll give you love
when I've climbed this stair.

Where are you hiding?
Deep in the wood.
I'll give you wood
when your bottom's bare.

Why are you crying?
I'm afraid of the dark.
I'll give you the dark
and I do not care.

Gavin Ewart

ANTHEM

Our bones will all be built into the runway
with the bones of the Chinese coolies who are building the
    runway
who are starving to death and are building the runway
so that the Japanese planes may take off over the ocean.
We too shall feel faint and fall down and be built into the
    runway
our bones will be powdered flat with the stones and
    squashed into the runway,
the bones are an indeterminate white that go into the
    runway,
there are no blacks or yellows or whites in the bones of the
    runway,
they are dry and chalky as the stones we build into the
    runway.
Each brings his stones and his bones for the path of the
    runway,
so that the Japanese planes may take off over the ocean.

HIGH POETIC CIRCLES

When poets get quite famous
they often like to say,
in a modest kind of way:
'I was talking yesterday to Seamus . . .'
'Philip says . . .', 'According to Peter . . .',
'Roy has invented a new metre . . .'

53

Ah, who runneth and who readeth!
It runs like a sitcom!
Once it was 'Yes, Tom
told me himself, and Edith . . .'
It's never 'So says my old pal Fred . . .'
but 'I *said* to Lord Alfred . . .'

So the names are always dropping –
Kit, Ben and Will
might have felt quite ill –
not rampant then? But old (and not stopping!).
The parasites in Rome cried 'Bacchus!
you *must* meet the poet Q. Horatius Flaccus!'

THE SADOMASOCHISTIC SATISFACTIONS OF SEAFOOD

Oh, they love the larky lobsters,
and the stiffness of the sturgeons,
the electric eels are thrilling,
and the swordfish cut like surgeons!

Oh, the sharks are sharp and shocking
and their tiger-teeth are topping,
and the narwhal, never nimbler,
passes through you without stopping!

Oh, the octopus is ogling
and his tentacles are tangling,
giant clams are quickly closing –
it's a special kind of angling!

Oh, the sea has many lovers,
that great ocean's truly tidal –
plunge right in and you'll die happy
if you're feeling suicidal!

Alastair Fowler

FITTING

You are pulling on my riding boot
High as a thigh-high boot, then higher,
Tight as I fit my high-heeled foot

Into the toe's extreme acute.
Strict to the last of your desire
You are pulling on my riding boot.

You are easing on my big-league boot
Smooth as the highest most dangerous wire,
Tight as I fit my high-heeled foot.

How will its cruelly close volute
Ever come off before I expire?
Now you have pulled my riding-boot
Tight. I fit my high-heeled foot.

LOVE'S PROMISES

For Christ's sake let me in.
I promise to be gentle and
Good as a mouse
If you let me in, and small.

Just let me come inside.
I'll be quiet as a horse

Of wood, and not move
Until you let me rock.

Let me in. I won't
Wolf you up or down:
Just nibble a bit
Like an innocent lamb.

(Unless a bouncing ram's
The thing you really want
To go on the batter,
To let go, in there.)

Don't be so cold and hard:
Don't let me freeze out here.
Inside, when I thaw,
I'll be hard, too.

OUR LOVE IS MADE, YOUR HEAVY HEAD . . .

Our love is made, your heavy head
Stacked in my arm's tired loop.
Leg by leg we sanctified husks
Lie easy and rest within
Our double niche. Calamities and
Cruelties may rage outside, beyond
This recess from worlds we toiled about
Once. We've done what lovers do;
Need do no more to show our love.

In the circle within the guard, inside
The inward pentacle of limbs – all holds
Unbarred to willing lovers – we allow
Whatever our remaining moods
Presume. That boundary of self
We feel as feeble or gone; yet know
Everything now is going well.
But how are we sure that elsewhere other
Divided souls will join as one?

In our clear indulgent trance we saw –
Before that tender love gave place
To new desire – the way it would
Be done. To begin, we'd pacify all
Our other borders. Peace from this bed!
We had only to stay in love: to keep
Our love for one; and be as warm
In other ways to others. Mankind
Would write the poem of love again.

But armies of difference crop up thick:
Tomorrow, today, we shall forget
How much we loved. Or the world will not
Respond. We shall fail. In the lapse of life,
Even our special flesh must fail –
Must fade and worse. Soon, maybe,
Only love will stand – but shall,
Having made, on this day of days,
An affirmance of being that nothing can annul.

Offering no safe conduct through,
No repetition, no continuance,
It promised only a single hope.
And for that, your sudden glow in love
Had only to transpire once, to give
The fairest idea of a paradise
The vital thread leads on towards.
From your sweetness then, I know the way
By ordinary love is not too long.

We are almost looking at still lifes. Flowers
Before they droop raise spirits and another point,
A further subject, between the pinks, about
Each petal. Beyond that fancy roemer of Kalf's
(Doubtful reflection) there's always a dark shade of it.
Swarthy sables from Brunswick and Frankfort make
Its pitch and we brush it, through the treacle glaze.
Mysterious dark without a verb. Elsewhere
Blue flags wave out brave messages how to face
Efflorescence's briskness. Fine; and now
Decipher black's. More perfect than colours, it sends
None. Is it one of a composition of tones
To concentrate the mind on the virtue of flowers
Wonderfully? An edge, a word limit,
It compresses them. But don't assume it's part
Of a second subject, as what the pinks must waste
Into, be translated to, when their life
Is quite still. Not that black, nor tones
Of black, are conditions of vivid pinks,
A necessary contrast. What if we learn to restore;
Choose to find that the night watch steps out
In broad day, that Kalf never meant
His shaded grounds as mystery. His only way,
Rather, to blot what could not yet be seen
By candle power. His black could still disclose,
Beneath the varnish, eight *natures* at least:
Vasefuls of pinks, convent gardensful of fruit,
Each with a word found, none a vanitas.
Or we could make the vacant dark a line,
Like the two-way vertical frame in comic strips –
Formal, unremarkable – leading on
To ordinary lives, other gallery views.

HAPPY

Overnight the bush had been cancelled
And new roughed in mist:
Hints of eucalyptus ghosts
And stone spaces – long walks
From firewood to firewood. But the breakfast fire
Could wait for an oddity. Not the dawn,
Lunar gray, nor the axe's magic,
Rebounding from the rubbery gumwood,
But Happy's patent leather shoes
Propped on the wire. His name came out
When I mentioned the brown merino sheep
By the gate, hooflets leant on the wire,
Begging like a bright poodle. It seems
He'd been reared as a pet, just to please
The shepherd's children. Year after year
Happy and his hopes were raised as one
Of the family, until his friends went off
To school and he had none.
Put out, he picked up again
With his woolly mates. They found him strange.
So he'd stand and yearn, while the sallow dawn
Grew bright enough to explain away
Fantastic promises of dew and gold.

TWO HUNDRED UNBORN LAMBS . . .

Two hundred unborn lambs were sacrificed
For one illuminated book: and thousands of trees
Fall, to put a paper once to bed.
I ask for more, yet less. In our natural life
We fill two zeppelins with air; but all
I beg of you is three short words – and they
Would mean so much that dictionaries then
Would not be enough to tell my exaltation.

THAT FABULOUS NEBULA . . .

That fabulous nebula all observe
May just be light that has travelled round
The universe – round and back to us –
From stars of our own, ages ago.
Like the brilliant girl I looked
Again at, in the street, who sparkled
As you did once, fizzlingly young,
And brought our first love home to me.

Geoffrey Grigson

THE CREMATORIUM

A grand advantage – and, if so,
To whom – to pile on a most high
Summit flaming logs, so visible from
Far off surrounding hills, also
From far out to sea, oak logs crackling
And what had been yourself, once,
Vanishing? Well, it argued you
Had known yourself powerful, certainly,
Important, rich; that others politically
Thought so too? Grand flames rose in the dusk,
Then fell, and in solemnity died down.

　　Now, friend, if you, or they, can pay – it's not
A grandeur of the dead you join.
That's sure. Dark limousines discreetly sneak
Into the somewhat secret Crematorium
Wood, off a side road outside our town.
Only oak leaves of autumn now fall down
In Crematorium Lane. Widows wear black,
Are secretly ashamed, and almost glad
You've gone. They disappear. Tired attendants
Turn their gas jets down; and yet between *B.*
C. and *Now* I guess that things are much the same.

Tony Harrison

PAIN-KILLERS

I
My father haunts me in the old men that I find
holding the shop-queues up by being slow.
It's always a man like him that I'm behind
just when I thought the pain of him would go
reminding me perhaps it never goes,
with his pension book kept utterly pristine
in a plastic wrapper labelled *Pantihose*
as if they wouldn't pay if it weren't clean,

or learning to shop so late in his old age
and counting his money slowly from a purse
I'd say from its ornate clasp and shade of beige
was his dead wife's glasses' case. I curse,
but silently, secreting pain, at this delay,
the acid in my gut caused by dad's ghost –
I've got aerogrammes to buy. My love's away!
And the proofs of *Pain-Killers* to post!

II
Going for pills to ease the pain I get
from the Post Office on Thursdays, Pension Day,
the chemist's also gives me cause to fret
at more of my dad's ghosts, and more delay
as they queue for their prescriptions without hopes
and go looking for the old cures on the shelves,
stumbling into pyramids of scented soaps
they once called cissy when they felt 'themselves'.

There are more than in the Post Office in BOOTS
and I try to pass the time behind such men

by working out the Latin and Greek roots
of cures, the *san*– that's in *Sanatogen,*
compounds derived from *derm*– for teenage spots,
suntan creams and lotions prefixed *sol*–
while a double of my dad takes three wild shots
at pronouncing PARACETAMOL.

CHANGING AT YORK

A directory that runs from B to V,
the Yellow Pages' entries for HOTELS
and TAXIS torn out, the smell of dossers' pee,
saliva in the mouthpiece, whisky smells –
I remember, now I have to phone,
squashing a *Daily Mail* half full of chips,
to tell the son, I left at home alone,
my train's delayed, and get cut off by the pips,
how, phoning his mother, late, a little pissed,
changing at York, from some place where I'd read,
I used 2p to lie about the train I'd missed
and ten more to talk my way to some girl's bed
and, in this same kiosk with the stale, sour breath
of queuing callers, drunk, cajoling, lying,
consoling his granpa for his granny's death,
how I heard him, for the first time ever, crying.

JUMPER

When I want some sort of human metronome
to beat calm celebration out of fear
like that when German bombs fell round our home
it's my mother's needles, knitting, that I hear,
the click of needles steady though walls shake.
The stitches, plain or purl, were never dropped.
Bombs fell all that night until daybreak
but, not for a moment, did the knitting stop.
Though we shivered in the cellar-shelter's cold
and the whistling bombs sent shivers through the walls
I know now why she made her scared child hold
the skeins she wound so calmly into balls.

We open presents wrapped before she died.
With that same composure shown in that attack
she'd known the time to lay her wools aside –

the jumper I open's shop-bought, and is black!

Philip Hobsbaum

LAST MEMO

E.M.Y., 11.9.83

A robin hurries through the quadrangle,
Chirps in the dusk. Now that I cannot utter
A word you'll hear about *The Cardinall*,
Your last meticulous text, I write this letter

Too late to say your wit cut through the weather
With fortitude more than the frame could shoulder –
You leave us well in autumn. You are spared the
Banality of growing old, and older.

A CREDENTIAL

They are picking off all my friends, one by one,
The hand in the embassy knows how to shoot straight:
One faces an eternity without sun,
Another by now knows there's no such state –

Barry, Martin, Beth, you are all gone
Into the dark, possibly into the light,
One cannot lie down before this, one cannot run,
I feel it upon my pulses, my friends' fate –

Whether by stealthy shot or punishing fire
We share a future more than ever a past,
Under the guns of the embassy ends desire,
Office and modesty thrown aside at last –
The sick man's jewel, the prisoner's release,
Under the guns of the embassy find our peace.

Michael Hofmann

ANCIENT EVENINGS

for A.

My friends hunted in packs, had themselves photographed
under hoardings that said 'Tender Vegetables'
or 'Big Chunks', but I had you – my Antonia!
Not for long, nor for a long time now . . .

Later, your jeans faded more completely,
and the hole in them wore to a furred square,
as it had to, but I remember my hands
skating over them, there where the cloth was thickest.

You were so quiet, it seemed like an invitation
to be disturbed, like Archimedes and the soldier,
like me, like the water displaced from my kettle
when I heated tins of viscous celery soup in it

until the glue dissolved and the labels crumbled
and the turbid, overheated water turned into more soup . . .
I was overheated, too. I could not trust my judgment.
The coffee I made in the dark was eight times too strong.

My humour was gravity, so I sat us both in an armchair
and toppled over backwards. I must have hoped
the experience of danger would cement our relationship.
Nothing was broken, and we made surprisingly little noise.

Like a man pleading for his life,
you put novels between yourself
and your pursuers – Atalanta,
always one step ahead of the game.

You gave me a copy of your second
with the dedication: *Michael,*
something else for you to read.
The casualness of your imperative

was too much resented for obedience . . .
You were a late starter at fiction,
but for ten years now, your family
has been kept at arm's length.

– We are as the warts on your elbows,
scratched into submission, but always
recrudescent. You call each of us
child, your wife and four children,

three of them grown-up. You have
the biblical manner: the indulgent patriarch,
his abused, endless patience; smiling
the absent smile of inattention . . .

Everything you need is at your desk:
glue-stained typewriter, match-sticks,
unravelled paper-clips – *Struwwelpeter* props!
With your big work-scissors, you snipe

at your nails, making the sparks fly.
The radio updates its bulletins
every hour, guarding you against surprises.
The living breath of the contemporary . . .

Once, you acceded to conversation,
got up to put on your black armband
and took your blood-pressure, as though
in the presence of an unacceptable risk.

Michael Horovitz

FOR LEON BISMARCK BEIDERBECKE (1903–1931)

    Bix's sound . . .

  – so often spoken of
  as bell-like

yet if you think of actual bells – how many
sound the least bit
Bix-like?

    It must be the perfect
    symmetry of form
    the very idea of
    a bell evokes

  . . . the unerringly   measured way
the clear notes   cascade and swell –
erupt, shimmer down   ripple and well
from the bell   of his angelic horn

  forever preserving   and extending
  its cloudless blue   outlines
  imploding   the air

  – Bye bye   white bird
  whose feather   finger'd breaths
like the plangent   dongs of campanology
caressed, yes   so subtly
drew out   those quicksilver
jewelled rounds   and still movements
unimagined inside
  creamy cornet   chop jelly

. . . whose bright flame beat a path
hard as blowtorch through mist
– the way through those precious
few nights, dark and light
you laid bare
   the blushing secret
   heart of each song

   blowing bubbles
   O the colours
   of all the jazz
   youthful ages

     that never die
     blown so high

      – perfect syllables
      of recorded time.

Anthony Howell

RAMBLE

Birch, hazel, oak, beech, holly,
I'm out for a walk while you're sitting
In this wonderful kimono your friend Shelley gave you;
Feeling like an Australian Japanese lady.

Hinds fade into ferns faded as foxes.
Ember-like outcrops match this bracken March.
As you write, my thoughts bed you in a gazebo:
Summerhouse dream-room to my winter hanky.

Scanners over airfields turn their azimuth
In quadrants all too far for weekend romances.
Stuck here, I discern among tree skeletons
The mulberry vapour of the silver birches.

I'm beset by such a storm of pent emotion
I could get my whole arm up that rabbit-hole;
Even worse, there's an earthy smell from the foxes.
Fists fuse in the sinewy handshake of beeches.

White snakes are the birches, peeling their skins off
Like slim courtesans who let the wrapper slip;
A pleasure to incline, because elastic;
Flimsy, with their mulberry mist uppermost.

There is no getting to the bottom of this.
It was over a week ago you were sitting there,
Writing, in black and silvery grey stripes,
Of the nice pattern on your new kimono.

Though I'd have sent my radar through the earth,

As you leant a bit forwards, and the fabric
Lifted up just to provoke me, you Australian
Japanese lady, my English Japanese birch.

BELMORE

Seek out a rill from the sound of its fall:
A sombre jar-glug, bottled up below
The crag whispering from top to toe
Of gauzy material trailed across the hill.

Hear all the tinkles on the little ledges
Choosing between assorted fans and plumes
Sheltering beneath a stand of giant gums
Shabbily tearing at the sky's edges.

Then from an outcrop of more rugged ground
Peer over larger waters pouring down
With the sound of many sheets being torn,
Heard or unheard according to the wind

As it enters or exits gateways through the rocks;
And you will learn what water knows of the puffs
And shuntings of engines, of the thousand wharfs,
And mineshaft machinery in that vaulted box

Of a wild cathedral, where from the pulpit
Mention of saws in timber-mills and planks
Being dropped in yards assures you water thinks
For humankind and how it can help it.

NUDES

Slow is the heart
To love what the eye cannot see.
The watcher notes the eternal light
Within the watched, the mortal being.
Great longing the only experience
Experienced under the warm white light:
The nude strolling, taut backs
Of the spirit knees
And stocky beginnings of calves.

Wonder of how things fit
Or are soft enough to permit us in there.
Nests of removable arms
Along the limbs, between bells.
Amphorae, shells, anemones.
Coverts and enclosures
Looking inward on themselves.
Their privacy is thus their protection.
The grapes seems swollen with light.

THE AGE OF THE STREET

Here is the passing of an uneventful hour
In a backwater of the town, above a backwater of the bay
Behind the containers brought to this faraway shore.
Wall to wall carpet, sweet smelling dust in the air,
The gloss of doors, each knob a scintilla of day,
Rackets and hats, glimpses of sash and pane
Through the blinds, flaws troubling the picture plane:
Then lengths of railing, kerb and the grey camber
Levelling off into gutters lead the eye away
With the newsboy's whistle as he tugs his trolley of papers

Up the shallow incline punctuated by some blooms.
An hour between darkness and light for overcast portions
Of changeable afternoons; monochrome, khaki and amber
Moments with no more definition than a reproduction
In the discarded volume: vacant chairs and rooms,
Reticent gardens, phones unanswered, pasted over heaven,
Locked factory gates. The blinds obey the suction
Or suspension of the breeze, exhale or hold their breath in;
Blinds gathered up or closing jerkily to obliterate
The criss-cross canvas view permitted through a mosquito
    net
Gridding the surface – before, or exhausted after
A storm out of season, watched through the slits in
    venetians.
A print smears the sheen of dust on an outer wing,
The texture of macadam alters, rain or shine,
As wobbly birds with a few feathers begin to sing
Wibbly-wobbly songs, and a weeping willow caresses
A Volkswagon in the otherwise uninhabited street.
Then a motorbike, or a girl casually shouldering tresses
Turns the corner, hardly in sight before gone
Past fronts incurious as to whether prompt or late.
Thinnish cloud, inconsequential wind, a sagging wire,
While a little colour is provided by the parked car.
Here, what's on the air is just preferred a little softer:
Loud noise-makers are locked behind factory gates.
Different hours obtain for dogs than do for cats.
Across the bay there's a stillness about the black lifter.

THE SQUIRREL

A rotten bale smouldering on a bonfire:
The caved in faces of aboriginals.
Images alien to the Hazeley woods:
Fires, floods, drownings, disappearances.

A remote continent floats away further
To the sound of thong-claps on an ocean liner,

Funnelling into one deeper blue
Fumes, mimosas, flowers and eucalyptus.

Plumes drift, stoked from below,
On horizons fixed at polarity's distance.
Off to its dray, that bushy tail
Keeping a treetrunk's girth between us.

OUT TOGETHER

It's quite a walk to where a bridge and stile
Straddle the Hart, at the edge of Hartley Wintney:
Getting there eventually, the body loosens;
Ease pervades the legs, the trunk,
The arms leaning against its rudimentary balustrade,
With a foot up against the lower bar.
We peer down at the weeds, and Quixotic tilts
Prang obviously as the rushes ebb
From the mind's reaches. Musings turn
To other matters. Here, at least for a while,
The brook wriggles across a water-meadow,
Dogs wag after water-rats holed in the bank's
Precipice, and the child babbles up
From beneath. 'Where does it go,
The little river? What have the dogs seen, Daddy?'
After a breather, there are the pigs
To see, and the sewage farm and the dump.
This last being Mecca for practical purposes;
Dragging a small arm or carrying
A lump dangling gumboots across a heath.

Michael Hoyland

FLUTE-PLAYERS

Someone went playing a flute
Down in the wet fields last night
Along the river, the moon
Wheeling out of the trees
With a slow whisper.

In that place, one haunted dusk,
A tall student, too, once stood
And played to a low light
In a small window till the call
Of the first quick thrush.

For my Scotch aunt Moll
There was no serenade.
Only this:
Pulling leeks in the rain,
She saw a man cross the road,
Pause at her gate and smile.
That proved
Her sole meeting with the god
In a life too long, she said.

Jenny Joseph

ONE THAT GOT AWAY

This little old lady I meet
Has nothing to do with poetry
Coming home late from work I pass her
Say once a week, maybe it's a Thursday.
She is entirely dressed in red
Not garish, though, not bizarre or fancy
And not at all a tramp.
Tiny, smart and silvered. She's still pretty.
I am going home from work, and she
Is coming from goodness knows what –
Pub, dustbins, cleaning – no knowing.
And I could not ask her.
She has nothing to do with poetry
And she has nothing to do with sociology.
Social workers may be out looking for her
To divide her into classes
Doctors to separate her into diseases
Politicians to flatten her into statistics
Poets to dispose of her in images.
She is not to do with any of that.
I did ask her once 'You all right, duck?'
First time I came on her, sat on a low church wall.
Surprised, she seemed – as if she wouldn't be all right!
She has nothing to do with horror stories or signs of the
    times.
Here she comes with her small packed carrier bag.
I am not going to tell you anything more about her.
She makes a track going here and there
Inhabitant.

A LETTER

Dear Friends
             Winter has come here.
It is not too bad as yet, though the darkness
Takes the centre, takes over, is beginning to make
Other things vague and futile. It
Is not all bad; the trees
Are sometimes very beautiful, it's just
It's sad Summer has left us. It's more difficult
To get done the things expected of us. That apart,
It suits me in a way. Perhaps
The slowness in the blood begins to suit me.
It lets you out – Winter – and I feel so lazy.
What can you do but let things go, in Winter?
I write these things to you in another country
Lest in fine weather you should sorrow for me
And wish me in another place. I soon will be;
Like you in a climate untouched by the seasons
Except in people's minds. The dead are unreached
By any of our changes and yet we think
Of you as minding that we think of you,
As bathed in sunlight, comforted by air.
I write to you, dear Friends, to let you know
That I am all right here, knowing often
Love and glad things I wouldn't have elsewhere
But turning, really, longing sometimes so strong
For my quittance, my papers, my number to come up
And set off for your country.
                        See you soon.

THE BALLAD OF RODBOROUGH COMMON

High on Rodborough
(Listen to my tale)
Stands an empty house
Commanding the vale.

Deep in grass on Rodborough
Two lovers lay
Sleeping murmuring fondling
The hours away.

Heavy in forgetfulness
The man slept;
To her house half down the dell
The woman crept.

Dog rose and elder flower
Pushed gutter high;
A light thrown on her ruined yard
Stopped her cry.

She crawled like a thief to her own back door
Hugging the wall
Two people sat at her table talking:
She heard it all:

> He dealt the cards 'What will you lay?'
> 'I've nothing left but my clothes,' she said.
> 'The clothes from off your back I'll play
> Against my holy love,' he said.

> He drew and won and had the clothes
> As she took them off her back, and then
> Fixing his shining eyes on hers
> 'I'll play you the light from your eyes,' he said.

> She drew and gasped. He took her light.
> 'What else will you give for love?' he said.

'I've nothing left but the skin on my bones.'
'I'll play for the bloom off your skin,' he said.

He drew and laughed and took her skin
And put it away in a box all folded.
'Clothes off your back, light from your eyes, bloom off
      your skin –
What next?' he said.

'The only thing that I've got left
Is what you've had long since,' she said.
'I'll give the blood that seeps from my womb
To get the other things back,' she said.

He drew and won. He took her blood
'And now I'll have the heart,' he said.
'I'll give you the heart from my body again
If you'll give me yours in exchange,' she said.

'My heart is made of words,' he said
As he dealt the cards for one more spate
'If I give it to you there'll be nothing there
In air it will evaporate.'

He played for her heart and wrenched it out
Of its place in her body 'and now,' he said,
'What have you left to give for love?'
'There is only the peace of my limbs,' she said.

He took her peace, and anguished and faint
She made a last plea and she drew her last bid
'To get my own love back again
I'll play you the strings of my mind,' she said.

He played. He won. Got up to go
Leaving her slumped in the chair as dead:
Hand on the kitchen door he turned
Not really listening to what she said.

'Give me a piece of your mind in return
For all the life you've taken,' she said.
'My mind is only a mirror made up
Of pieces out of yours,' he said.

'You have had the joy from my eyes,' she said,
'The bloom from my skin, the skin from my bones
The guts from my belly, the clothes from my back
The peace from my body, my heart from its rest
You have taken all these and thrown them away.
Are you giving me nothing back?' she said.

'Give me at least my mind again
Which you do not want, which you cannot use
That with it I can grow again
Skin, bloom, light, breath and get once more
All things thereto to make me live.
Give me back my sense again
To see and do the truth,' she said.

'That's not the way the game of love
Is played,' he said. 'I did not play
With you,' she said, 'and that you know.'
'Of course,' he said, 'and that is why
I chose to play the game with you.'

The watching woman found her way
Sick and shaking to the place
They had picknicked and played and slept, and she saw
The man from their house in her lover's face.

The food she had brought him she let fall
And the cover to keep him from the night air.
Shaking and sick she went over the hill
That sheltered the man still sleeping there.

Now elder stems grow
Through a broken chair
In a house standing empty
On Rodborough.

A WISH

Tears from long ago
Why come now?
Now with the birds singing
Now with the earth greening?

Tears long exploded
Why tick now?
Now with the sky clear
Now with friends near?

Bearable to think of cold, perhaps
When it is warm
And safe to give a little poke at horrors
That do no harm?

Child who shakes at fears
Which twenty years ago
Dried out when daylight came
Leaving only a stain
A bubble burst on the road

Child who creeps to my arms
Powerless, really, as yours,
Keep the gift of tears
Don't belittle fears.

May you always be
Among people who can say:
Tears from long ago
You can come now
Now that birds sing
And choking dust turns green.

P.J. Kavanagh

Words in the air, heard
Because they were spoken aloud
When I did not intend to speak,
Hang in the air like smoke.

I was visiting your grave,
Remembering you alive,
Of course, with the sense we have
That death is impossible;

Admiring again the girl-
Courage, trapeze-grace
That launches itself in space
Because it likes a face.

The world could not go on
Without the valour of women.
A thin young man, rufous,
Poor, with faults enough,

Then trusted with your life
Now moved to the church (Mary's).
Returning past your grave,
Is stopped, amazed to hear,

As though you stood there,
His words cleansed of grief:
'*God, you were brave!*'
His admiration pure,

Involuntary as a cough.

Patient bones in a sack,
Barely a mound beneath
The sheet, your rasping breath
Gives me childhood back:
Our quiet pictures when
You were all I knew
Unreel – but then on screen
Something I never called you,
A girl I never saw
Appears: Agnes O'Keefe,

And your brothers dead in the War
Two generations ago
Laughing, welcoming you.
As though this was the life
You needed to return to,
And I an interlude
Between your girlhood grief
And brothers who understood
Agnes, little Agnes.
Not my childhood, yours.

But how did that projectionist
With unremembered archive
Film arrive?
You may have expected this.
The patient bones of a tree
Wrapped in white mist
Suddenly touched by sun
Given colours again
Seem to expect no less.

But for a jackdaw's shadow
That crossed my feet in snow
I wouldn't have looked and seen
A sky-green horizon.
Self-preoccupation
In a lonely bird at dawn,
Strong-shouldering, intent,
Reminded me of mine
Staring down at snow.
Raised my eyes to space –
A black tree, a sky green –
I could not invent.
Gave me, nearly, grace.

Jean Hanff Korelitz

THE PROPERTIES OF BREATH

I. Descending the Lung

Hand over hand we inch. Our grips
are fine hairs, moving
in their tides. We sink
from rung to coated rung, until
it broadens out: a landscape, arcing
to the edges of the body. Looking
over shoulders we can see it: lung,
translucent mine, its dim. We cannot
move our feet for the mire the smoke makes.

II. Burning the Property

Smoke wakened us; the field
sloping up to the stone wall filled
with it, the filaments
of our neighbour's grasses flying.
Shovels and boots: our heels
brought his seedling flames back
to the earth, making them
black ash, a thick
scar at the field's rim.

Later, when the smoke had stilled, our neighbour
scattered ashes from his cigarette. He stubbed it
in the black, remarking
how it hardly mattered now. His chest
expelled itself. The property
would be more fertile, he decided, for that burn. We eyed
his steaming streaks, those tumors
on the lung of his slopes.

III. The Properties of Breath

These are the patches we circumvent, their pools
of dark. They list the properties of breath;
involuntary, breeding, burned. Tonight
our cigarettes smoke end to end, drawn down
to settle in that dim. What things grow here
we do not tend or till.

Our lungs expel themselves. We trap
what comes up, call it poetry.

B.C. Leale

THE RAT

the rat throws out all rattish thoughts
scaling a church's organ-pipes
sublime with Bach

the rat has this knowledge
he's not a pigeon a wasp or a tiger

if his teeth are gripping a windpipe
his mind's on a painting by Poussin

the rat is tearing the psychoanalyst's couch to pieces
& gnawing the walls of the empty labyrinth

the rat confronts in the blackness & brilliance of a mirror
the fraught lineaments of a whiskered Beethoven

RENDERINGS & SUNDERINGS OF COBBETT'S
RURAL RIDES

galloped from the hanged men on the swaying moors
the angry skies un-
sweetened by a touch of sun
trotted up to the well-baked risings
of the Yorkshire pudding
having shrugged off the quags & quicksands
& whipped away miserable hills
set my compass on the turnips & swedes
cantered up to their earthy favours
reined in on the hot juicy sides
of roast beef with its draperies of horse-
radish ensconced myself within a nook of
fumed oak quaffed
the incomparable claret
took my teeth
to the crackers & crumbling
cliffs of the Gorgonzola
smelt in the moulds of its cracks
the worm & the gibbet

Christopher Logue

COMA

Before he turned to stone
Atlas became the father of Calypso.

      'Kiss my toes!
      Kiss the back of my knees!'

Gozo was her inheritance. Behind its surf
by promising to rubbish time, she kept
a witty killer yearning for his wife
for longer than it takes
light to connect a human to a star.

Too bad for her he had a voice in Heaven

      'Now my wrist!
      Now my neck!'

for once restored to death he steered
a square beneath a triangle away
leaving her sleepless.

      'Father, I will go mad.'
      'We Atlases do not go mad,' he said,
and begged Creation to disarm her grief.

Even the strong have rights. So on the nod
Boy Hypnos came and kissed her pain away,
and Coma was their child.

FOOTNOTE

'Elderly mermaid, I sneeze in your lasagne',
damp has destroyed the rest of the page.

THE AARDVARK

Into the moonlit midnight,
out of his stateless hole,
set for an insect intake
a common aardvark stole.

Depict this common aardvark:
globe eyes of fiery rose;
long of tail, of tongue, of ear;
yet longer still of nose.

He sniffs the ermine moonshine;
he hears the vermin snore;
brisk as a whip the aardvark's tongue
streaks from the aardvark's maw . . .

GIGANTIC LICK SNUFFS GLOW-WORM!
MIDGE-CLOUD ENGULFED MID-AIR!
followed by half a thousand ants
(an aardvark's normal fare),

a myriad of rotifers
cruising a humid nit,
another half a thousand ants
(to keep him fat but fit),

an ounce of infant locusts,
a cache of millipedes,

91

another half a thousand ants,
and then? – ah, then he needs

rest on the trek through hunger
to woo his mortal soul.
Meekly the common aardvark
goes back into his hole.

MELISSIMA'S WALTZ

Music by Stanley Myers

To the consternation of his guests, Field-Marshall 'Plumbago'
Hardy (93) seizes Melissima Jones (16) and sings as they dance:

Slow, slow, Melissima.
When I was underdone
women encrinolined fled the ground,
fifty had just begun.
Eyelash and amethyst gathered the candlelight,
ivory beamed through lawn;
the music, Melissima, started at dusk,
and we danced until dawn.

Post! Post! Melissima!
Meadowsweet fledged with rain;
Twilight delighted by china dawn;
Paradise found in vain.
Snaps of antiquity fetched from Elysium,
merely a glimpse between;
my head may be grey, Melissima,
but my heart is still green.

TO MY NOW DISTANT BUT ONCE MUCH LOVED
FRIEND, *Mr Michael White, on the completion of* Empty
Seats, *the first volume of his autobiography. Written on the day
I received his postcard, saying: 'The food on Saint-
    Barthélémy is much better than the food in Bermuda.'*

I live a life of almost total idleness.
My friends grow silent.
My enemies rejoice.
But luckily my mind is fogged
by vanity and pride,
so I see nothing.
'Alas, my son,' my mother says,
'your case is hopeless . . .'
Her cheekbones glisten in the neon dusk.
'Unhook your ear and blow your nose, old bag,' I say –
but only to myself.

LIT. CRIT.

'If we were fucking,
and I suddenly wanted to write something down,
would you be angry?'
'No.'
'But would you suck my cock while I wrote it?'
'That depends on the words.'

George MacBeth

A BASKET OF WALNUTS

Night after night, I crack
One open, find
It rotten. Some dry lack
In toughened rind
Afflicts their taste.
The flavour sickens, and
It seems a waste.
Crushing one in my hand,

I try again. The shell
Breaks, and the brain
Inside it seems to swell
Or shrink, in pain.
Fantasy. But
Such ideas hurt the heart.
I crack each nut,
Anxious for a new start.

REMEMBERING MINCEMEAT

Day after day the sticky mixture stayed.
The bowls it lay in kept cool on grey marble,
Each with a spoon sucked in, as though a spade.

A wooden spoon. The clay of earthenware.
The mixture pummelled out of dough and spice
And apples by the plough-spoon like a share.

A share of earth. And water from the well.
Then subtle seething in the sough of mincemeat.
And something dark, peculiar, in the smell

As if the candles or the drains gone stale
Fermented, and then left a residue,
A tacky resin bitter as an ale.

This was the body we would eat in sorrow.
I knew each night and went to sleep so knowing.
And woke from dreams, tasting the dark tomorrow.

Norman MacCaig

OVER AND OVER AGAIN

Tomorrow we'll meet again
as for the first time, though we've not crossed
the river that's both kind and cruel –
that Lethe the ancients spoke about.
And of the buried suns one will arrive
and make bright the fields
where Persephone must have passed:
so many the flowers.
We'll not shrink when we skirt
the entrance to the Underworld
nor be blinded by that shell sauntering in
and Aphrodite stepping from it
on to the shore of everywhere.

All myths, with the truth of myths.
We'll do it our way –
with a look, with a touch
and with the space between words
where the truths hide
that we can find no words for.

ON THE NORTH SIDE OF SUILVEN

The three inch wide streamlet
trickles over its own fingers
down the sandstone slabs
of my favourite mountain.

Like the Amazon, it'll reach the sea.
Like the Volga
it'll forget its own language.

Its water goes down my throat
with a glassy coldness,
like something suddenly remembered.

I drink
its freezing vocabulary
and half understand the purity
of all beginnings.

A MAN WALKING THROUGH CLACHTOLL

He carries a scythe, but he's young,
he doesn't notice symbols.

Packs of waves hold the Split Rock at bay.
He pays no heed to their growling and slavering.

He's thinking of Mairi at the dance tonight.
She's his Aurora, she's his Merry Dancer.

They'll whirl in and out of six other lives and end
teetotuming alone. By God, they'll Strip the Willow.

He turns into the field and sets to work.
He rejects symbols. But he is one all the same.

And the hay falls and the dances end.
And the scythe cuts, no matter who's holding it.

BY THE GRAVEYARD, LUSKENTYRE

From behind the wall death sends out messages
That all mean the same, that are easy to understand.

But who can interpret the blue-green waves
That never stop talking, shouting, wheedling?

Messages everywhere. Scholars, I plead with you,
Where are your dictionaries of the wind, the grasses?

Four larks are singing in a showering sprinkle
Their bright testaments: in a foreign language.

And always the beach is oghamed and cuneiformed
By knot and dunlin and countrydancing sandpipers.

– There's Donnie's lugsail. He's off to the lobsters.
The mast tilts to the north, the boat sails west.

A dictionary of him? – Can you imagine it?
– A volume thick as the height of the Clisham,

A volume big as the whole of Harris,
A volume beyond the wit of scholars.

DARK CENTRE

The dust silvers and a wind from the corner
brings a dream of clarinets
into the thick orchestra. There's a place
sending messages across the river of people;
and the sullen wharves of buildings
begin to smell of bales and distances.

I have a sad cave where nobody enters
but a ragged man hooking the air
with skinny fingers. I sit beside him sometimes,
feeling his despair. His loneliness
infects me.

But today's a day of clarinets and silver
under the lucky horseshoe of the sky.
I leave him and go into the whirlpools of light,
through a jazz of gardens and heliograph windows.

That house is my cell, my fortress.

I put the key in the door and stop,
terrified that the ragged man
is sitting in my chair with his skinny fingers
tangled in his lap.

MEMORY

Over the turbulence of the world
flies the bird that stands for memory.
No bird flies faster than this one, dearer to me
than the dove was to Noah – though it brings back
sometimes an olive branch, sometimes
a thorny twig without blossoms.

Joan McGavin

TORN-WORD*

The torn-word dozes at the root of the tongue,
bides its time, is conformable among
chat, and platitudes, and love-sounds
that do not know it's different; while round
uncurls the torn-word, syllables long.
In a sibilant sortie its carefully pronged
fangs poise themselves to slake
with gall and wormwood
the wound they first make.

*Old English: a contemptuous or scornful word; a word intended
to cause distress.*

Angus Martin

GRANDFATHER

Grandfather's boat is out tonight.
The sea is galloping along beside her.
The sea has a simple sense of fun.
Nobody ever understood the sea.

He is an old man now, my grandfather.
Everybody thought that he was putrid.
Maybe he got restive underground.
He wanted a smoke and just got up.

The lights were strange around him,
but he sniffed the wind and came to.
He was seen determined on the trashy shore.
He was seen efficient at the fouled moorings.

The town woke up to the crack of a sail
and grandfather was steering out beyond the living,
his whiskers probing the chancy dark,
antennae of an indomitable patriarch.

They are in the storm together, boat and man,
ripping water on their final voyage.
My grandfather has no mind for herrings.
He scans the smoking runs of ocean.

He forgot that he had no future.
He raised himself and wandered,
in the roaring night of a world disordered,
to the mouth of the summoning sea.

He has gone, that exceptional corpse,
at peace on an unreturning tide,
out from the land that could not hold him
and the furious howl of his grave abandoned.

I LAUGHED WHEN THE PAINTER, CAROLINE

I laughed when the painter, Caroline,
delicately balanced on her nineteen years,
assured me that poets were obsessed with death:
she hated my pictures of drowned cats.

Today, on a frozen mountainside,
her solemnity tunnelled out to me
from the seized brain of a carcass,
a goat once, prancing on the roof of the world.

What lives and moves disorders the universe.
A rock dislodged by a foraging goat
falls out of place and tries its weight in air.
It leaves behind a hole in the earth, a silent vacuity.

Death too is silence, and must detain the poet:
the end of his art is lodged in it.
So, I looked today on death, and looked on silence,
a goat that was in the world, yet knew no part of it.

Immobile on iced immobility of mountain,
it was itself its final alteration
of the eternally altering vastness
of moveable earth and stone.

BAIT-GATHERING

That was the coldest of mornings.
My father broke ice
on the pools of the shore,
waiting for ebb.
He had gone too early,
descending the foot-sculpted stairs,
down from his attic bedroom,
bearing no light that winter morning,
a small boy dragging a wicker creel with him.

His father stirred him,
old Duncan, squat and muscular,
smelling of tar and fish,
and for thirty years obdurate
at the helm of his own skiff,
his pride as bright to the end
as superlative yacht varnish.
His hand, as hard as barnacles,
and longer tried by common elements,
touched his son who quivered in sleep,
some innocent dream alive in him.
'It's time,' was all he said.
My father woke, and time was in his mouth.
He dressed in the chill room,
and his shadow danced for him
fantastic on a wall.

He broke ice and kicked at darkness.
His basket tipped on its side
and rocked on the bared ebb stones.
Soon he would pack it up with mussels,
with frozen hands unfastening them,
a child's tears filming his eyes,
that fisherman's son, torn from his sleep,
as a living fish, in its shell of grace,
is riven from water.

Tomas O Canainn

NUALA'S FIDDLE

In Boston, Mass.
My daughter fingers notes
On a fiddle
My grandfather played
In Derry: her reels dance
Along over-grown paths
Once cleared by his bow.

Deep in my father's grave
My mother hid music
So her children did not know
She could draw a bow like the rest.

'A pity', she said to my playing,
'A pity we didn't buy
Thon wee fiddle o' the Gormans that time –
And you'd not be saddled now
Wi' them oul' pipes.'
But I knew
Chanter – like bow –
Would find its own path.

Years cover-up the players
But tunes remain:
Old notes from a bow
Re-form on pipes
And echo on fiddle again
In Boston, Mass:
Chanter or bow is a baton
To take for a turn
And pass.

Stephen Plaice

THE GHOSTS OF THE VICTORIANS

For her they were all in the future.
'Who is that gentleman in the morning room
tinkering with the tip-tap machine?'
Elly often frowned over one eye
and said things like this unnaturally
when they were quiet upstairs
and I had time for my needles.
'Isn't that the tube, Elly?' I said and she went.
But then it quickened.
'Nineteen eighty-five, six, who'll live here then?
The Nabob of Krishnapur and his seven wives,
the Admiral of Her Majesty's balloons,
the inventor of the speaking lines . . .
It won't be no Davenports for sure,
their breath is as short as a thimble.'
'Elly', I said, 'That's no way to talk in service.'
She was church-quiet, but then the frown came again.
'Who is that lady in the morning-room
squinting at the click-clack machine?'
'Mrs Fanshawe', I whispered in the pantry,
'that girl will be in Cold Harbour before the sloes are ripe.'
But it was the Fever took her.
The Doctor closed the frowning eye,
wiped his hands and said, 'From that incestuous clan
of monkeys out at Storrington.
Too many dark nights and daughters.'
He was a clever man the Doctor,
his linctus took away my cough,
but did nothing for Elly or Davenports alike.

I saw her once afterwards,

the day the youngest Master died,
she still had that frown over one eye –
'Elly', I said, 'does it hurt you still?'
She pointed upstairs. The tube whistled.
I went. He was dead. She was right.
Since then the charabanc, the aeroplane,
telephone, electric light,
Mrs Fanshawe could no longer manage the stairs.
Now the Mistress is dead. The Doctor is dead.
Old Mr Davenport has a bell beside his bed.
The tube whistles sometimes in the middle of the night.
The children, bless them, still love a game.
For me, they are all in the past.
I remember over my needles how Elly once said –
'Nobody really lives here any more,
we are already safe, at home, on the farm.'
I like to think of us there, all of us,
not here any more, not in this house
I will be the last to forget.

MELANCHOLIA

Girls, under this tree where you sit observed,
tittering, sipping your bright lemonade,
Melancholia sat, heavy with her third son,
as yet unnamed, but destined for the church
unless the first grew sickly and the second fell.
Of all the Earl's stately trees she preferred
this copper beech, a sport as yet unnamed,
sat there with open book, closed parasol
on sunlit days when the leaves grow darker
and from a distance smoulder against the greens.
Above her the grey convoluted branches rose,
an allegory of the swollen roots below.

All through August, and in her eighth month,
the gardener brought her a daily offering
rolling in his flat trug – a single lemon,

the first the orangerie had grown.
She waited for his shadow to lengthen,
modestly, as one about to disrobe,
and then, though his gaze was still upon her,
she gnawed greedily at the zestful rind
so the juice ran, staining the pages.
With puckered lips and unfamiliar teeth,
she sucked long on the bitterness in the belief
this time she succoured her God-given girl.

It was late September when her waters broke,
she refused the doctor and his sweet phials –
'I will see no man but the gardener',
she confided to the maid. The gardener came
bringing the last sharp fruit as if by design.
'The English summer does not suffice to sweeten him,'
he appeared to say, looming tall at her feet,
his beard seething with bees like a honeycomb.
Later the Earl came muddled with claret,
his veins etched as clear as the back of a leaf.
'Do not be angry with me', she heard herself speak,
'I am carrying the gardener's child.'

A smell of camphor on the stairs.
The boy was delivered on the sopping sheet
and God took his mother in exchange.
In the scullery the maid set him to her breast,
as she had done his brothers before.
The gardener crept back to peer through the crack,
with his eye upon her, she felt at peace,
but fear at night with no one watching
as a crapulous hand fumbled at the latch
and rough whiskers scratched the nape of her neck.
October mornings staking out the sheets in the wind,
she saw Melancholia musing beneath the black tree.

The first grew sickly, the second fell,
the Earl's estate came down to the third,
thin as a winter reed, fox-faced, feminine,
more suited to the cloth, the village said.
In summer he browsed in the orangerie
with only marble Nausicaa to play ball –
the gardener long since back in the Downs.

In winter, as a man, he shared the sculptor's longing
for his homeland's more definite light,
with number and symbol, hermetic device,
he sought in the night the elixir of life,
but thirty English summers sufficed.

Girls, under this tree where you sit observed,
Melancholia sat with her pitcher of tears,
till the green-streaked stone blended into the garden
and her meaning was lost on its inheritors.
They dragged her with chains then back to the house.
You may go to her now, that door is open,
or you may rest here under the gardener's gaze,
never wondering what brought you out in the light.
Even now that all is named and the lemon cheap,
from a distance, most girls seem to choose this tree,
till the shadows touch and beauty streaks.
Then they rise up and go inside.

FAREWELL, MY LATIN MASTER

That afternoon where the yellow light,
not sodium yet, glowed warm inside,
eyes down, scoring our boredom on the desks,
we leant, one elbow planted, one ear cocked
ready to receive the wisdom of the classics,
you gave us Juvenal, over bi-focals,
construed that passage with a halting catch,
the one you said no one forgets:
'*Farewell. Remember me. When Rome returns you
eager for rest and peace to Aquinum, ask me
from Cumae to visit you, and your Ceres and your Diana.
Unless your satires are ashamed of me, I'll stride
in heavy boots through your cool fields to hear them.*'
A few of us stiffened, raised our heads
as if we suddenly scented clean air outside,
the satchel-tossing freedom of summer fields.

Indeed I am tired of London,
of friends bickering in half-paid houses,
bored with the partners they barely scratched,
sleeping in whatever bed seems warmest
and already dreaming of the next.
My dreams, no better, seduced by naked holographs
of the listless Swiss telephonists in my class
who sit considering their spectacular nails
while I am side-tracked to satirize my past.
But now sometimes, saying goodbye to them, I hear the
    catch,
fight the tears of which school first disabused me,
as Juvenal and your voice comes back:
'*Farewell. Remember me. When Rome returns you . . .*'
But then I have to go and look it up.

Farewell, my Latin master, and rest assured,
a few of us have not forgotten this much,
though Rome, Berlin, the Pound have fallen,
but not yet the Bomb, at least on us.
In the white light, should you return one afternoon,
you will find us grown yellow and cantankerous,
in heavy boots, urging our flocks of Eurogeese along
to honk by rote the Past Continuous you called Imperfect
so that they might somehow pass the echo
of the echo of that midnight warning on.

Sacha Rabinovitch

LIPOGRAM

I rank fifth in a list. Again
in a list I follow what's first.
Though of woman I'm only a third,
of man I am half. I am last
in our transit from birth to our tomb,
and I'm first and I'm third
in that plot of man's fall.
I am part of that vast liquid mass
which transports us abroad
and sounds through our days and our nights.

But I'm not in our land or our sky,
I'm not in our light giving sun,
in our moon or our stars.
And I'm not in this lyric.

For things immediate
for actual love and hate
books were the surrogate.

I slaughtered on his knees
brave Hector to appease
the anger of Achilles,

seared out the single eye
of Cyclops in his stye
yet wouldn't hurt a fly.

No woman that I'd seen
could vie with Albertine
or with Leontes' Queen,

and if I knew desire
it was what fed the fire
of Dido's funeral pyre.

My heart sincerely bled
for tears Francesca shed
when Hell's winds buffeted,

but with indifference I
ignored my neighbour's cry.
And life has passed me by.

Simon Rae

BUCOLIC

---

*'Non cogito, ergo sum felix is the fundamental apophthegm,
aphorism or what-not of the rustic philosophy.'*
Aldous Huxley to Lady Ottoline Morrell

We lead a boorish existence out here
in the sticks. Away from the discipline
of architecture, our minds grow birdsnesty;
far from the classical beauty of the galleries,
our aesthetic sense dulls
to an appreciation of beefy flanks
or a perfectly ploughed furrow. Unrelieved
by the opera, our criminal passions
ferment like the hot chemicals of a silage clamp.

But we like it here, with mud on our boots,
sweat in our shirts, beer in our guts,
and nothing but a few idle birdsongs
rubbing together like twigs between our ears.

THE CATALOGUING

I watch the hands which once beat iron
round the blunt rhino horn of an anvil
and hit the safe nails home, placably filing
a nail-paring's purchase on blackened metal
for me to scratch a blobby number on.

He seems unconcerned at what time has done,
the face under the cap intent on his task,
or, when he looks up, brightly smiling.

We work at our own pace, the file
nagging the silence, my wretched nib
catching and spluttering on the ringwormed steel.
Visitors drift in and look around.
'Females' he'll challenge with weird shapes,
teasing with facetious hints before enacting
passage through soil, or vaguely phallic couplings
of bolt and bracket, trace-hook and harness.

Later inside for me, he holds up each
newly numbered piece. I catechize
according to the cataloguing sheet: name,
other name, material, period/date; where
made, 'Provenance Used', and special marks.
We tilt chisel blades to make out '. . . effield . . . GLAND'
or try the schoolboy trick of rubbing paper
held firmly over indentations with a pencil.

Some things he made himself as prentice work;
others go back more than a hundred years.
He lets me hold two swages in my hand:
their cold black weight is packed as tight as ice,
though forged in fire. Rivets of England,
they pin a handshake from the past into my palm.
I hand them back, then type: 'Used in the forge
for punching axe-head holes or shaping rods . . .'

Then, when we've done for the day,
he takes his spectacles off and folds them away.
Repressing the thought: 'Material, glass lenses
in plastic frame, metal case with the linen
worn at one corner', I pack up my portable.
Still talking, he sees me out to the car.
'Same time next week, Mr Gibbard?' I say
through the wound-down window. He nods and waves.

GENTLE GHOSTS

I watch you packing the past
back into its two respective diaries,
alternative photograph albums:

junk, pictures, too many books.
I help with the film cliché share-out
of a hundred LPs, after which

we take the old bedstead down
to the Municipal tip – that
repository of domestic failure,

sad, yet strangely titillating,
like a row overheard involuntarily
through the bedroom wall.

We lug the heavy head-board
over to the yawning refrigerators.
I feel a sudden, tender frisson,

startled like Adam on Eden's empty
threshold, seriously tempted
to make a pass at Eve.

DRAINING THE ORNAMENTAL LAKE

The steps step into light,
slipping off the currents' gentle intimacies.

The stone lip lapped by the punt's wash
slowly dries; supporting brickwork
inches into air.

114

Daily we watch
the water's stagnant wasting,
peering expectantly into the shrinking depths,
eager for dead men's shoes,
lovers' twined skeletons weighted
with a cupid's head, the spilt cargo
of an antique picnic basket . . .

Instead of giving back our questing faces
with sympathetic branches, cloud-patterned sky,
the mud base rises like the roof
of an ascending lift. Half a century's sediment
has sieved down to this silted sump
littered with the collapsed parachutes
of water lilies, corroded masonry,
a solitary jar.

The last inches trawl a desperate fry.
The shallows glut and pulse
as the net dips and spills.
A huge carp slaps itself in a batter of mud,
is pancake-raced away on a shovel.

Post-deluge geographies emerge
around the drain: a delta basin,
mottled mudflats laced with serpentine tricklings
winking in the astonished sunlight.

And Venus, reclining on her stone chaise-longue,
becomes accessible to suitors –
if anyone should take the necessary
slurry-nudging strides
to claim her bland, eroded features.

Peter Redgrove

SOME LOVE

Loving the watery stairs
Descending from the towpath,
Their thin loose treads,
Their slipping threads,
The sipping stairs
Like lighted rungs
With sky in them,
The slapping treads
Uttering in low voices;
In the leafy park by the towpath
The green-painted benches
Ranged like a theatre of the trees
Comfortably arrayed to witness
The dramatic slow leafing over decades,
And above us the sketchbook of the clouds
Designing parks, to view the river-locks,
Sash-windows of water sliding
Where the bubbling key
Opens the lock, the boiling key,
Ranged like a staircase up the river,
A wooden staircase lifting to the source,
The water-lifts hoisting the barges,
The yachts, as on silver trays
Up to the higher reaches, nearer the source:
You, Sir! in your silver-mounted yacht,
Your brightwork; and you, Sir!
In your barge heavy and thick
As useful fruitcake; the dark barges wading deep
With heavy coal, the white
Angel-yachts scudding almost empty.

NOT MACHINES

The insects have a speculative gaze
Like a bowl of diamonds.
They are not machines,
The river shaking out along its path
Green canopies of leaves and bugs,
Little capsules with strong dark eyes
Leaping in gauzes out of dungcakes,

The river sailing between live trees
As if the water travelled under sail,
These masts towering over me
As I navigate to the source,
Towering over me like branching rivers,
Maps standing on their source,
The insects still flowing past in multitudes,
Gongs of ooze, ringing bells of mud,
Wet bread of earth with voices at song,
An infinite scripture made of insects
Like a papery scroll flowing past,

And the tree a thin tissue scrolled
Over its last of yesteryear wood,
Tissue soaked in syrup-of-insect,

They assemble on the bark and drink
At their fountains of green sugar-blood,
The waxy triquiremes, the resurrectors
Slicing the roofs out of their pearly huts,
The dust of eggs mapped in villages
On the banks of the flowing green-leaf rivers,
The domed intersections of this world
With that singing one, singing of sun
That warms the syrups that then sprout wings,

The spindly convalescents of the egg
Feeling their shaky way on crooked sticks,
The launching out on skin-thin wings

With the glistening eyes of convalescents
In tears of joy as they fly, their crutches
Welded to their shoulders, fused to their bones,
Gangsters with glittering gazes,
Their guns fastened to their faces,
Images
Blown into the rain and granted wings
If the sun shines, the trees

Great wooden stoves of water-flame
Instead of fire, the green smoke
Stepping up in leafy valances and the pollen
Flaring out of the bushy stove-top, the river
Burning without a flame, the water rising
In a cold smoke that turns to rain
Which is a fire that flames downwards
And in the downpour
The staved trunks are stout barrels
Sudsing with green beer
And with barrel-bellied flies strapped in their segments,
Stout drinkers, winged vats
In the droning barroom of the carcass
Stacked with cell-bottles in rows and ranks
Where the loungers buzz as they sip,
Resurrectors and transformers but not machines
And with never-closing eyes like diamonds
And with unblinking eyes like spirits;

And flocks of orange dry flat flies
Rustle in the barn store and burst out
Of the high loft door like exploding sacks,
And the carcass a busy junction,
The porters lugging ragged leathers,
The spirits flocking on new journeys,
The vivid uniforms of the railway people,
The sounds of locomotives revving up,
The winged spirits in their holiday clothes
Which are their adult imago,
The evolvers who remain unevolved,
The elder forms who do not need to change,
As if the wheels were known to be the watchmakers,
The bronze flies humming like gongs
And shining like the sun-god;

I am brought out by many-jointed midwives
Packed with their musty honey, the living tunes,
Out of the tree I sip its cloudy syrups
Of my glittering nursery, and sit
Wide-eyed with my glee like diamonds. Proteus,
Multi-faceted Proteus
Hold still awhile, pouring your diamonds.

A WORLD

The world full of sugar and rain
Rubs up against us with its muzzles.
The hanging lamps of convolvulus
Shedding scent like radiance, like
Reading-lamps of black light
That is perfume, the snail
Fastened to the stem reads its scroll
From inside, with black light.
The wooden click or tock
As the fertile cone drops, the wood
Ticking like a wooden clock
As the timber roses drop,
The cogged pine-cones
Full of yellow honey and
Cough-drop gums, lung-healing balsams
In the wet pine-forest smelling like a
Healing sickroom, some gigantic person
Recovers himself among balsamic odours
And white sheets of water; I can see
With rinsed, convalescent eyes
As the odours roll down the vistas
Like gigantic nurses in headdresses;

The tree shedding its mirror down its trunk,
Glistening balsams, where the big-bummed aphids
Feed like drops of the fat river, like tuns,
Like cisterns brimming with green medicines,
Like articulated tankers transporting green serums,

Or Aesculapian galleys rowing with many legs,
Or stout pots of herbal tea,
Their eyelash-legs finer than razor cuts,
The sap of a wounded tree still walking,
Cauldrons of green glass on staggering stumps,
The portly Green Man in an insect-mask.

THE APPRENTICE AT THE FEAST

The wooden hives sealed with a glue of propolis,
Sealed and resealed in an instant by those busy claws
And tooled-up mouths. The Beemaster, mild in his age,
    shows
How the honey gathers in the hive-top, in the head of it,
And may be harvested, for the Queen passeth not to lay
Due to certain gates too small for her, but her workers go
In and out, brimming the six-sided cells with shining honey.

The feast of metheglin and honey served
On the shores of Furnace Ponds, and people sit
Gay with fantastic paper streamers
Pinned to their clothes, and the wind
Rushes up and down between the emptied houses
That drum in their wooden attics. Stories are told,
The boy listens open-mouthed, he has heard them before,
His back prickles with light hairs like a golden mist.

The wickerwork and tar is set alight,
It is a ball of flame kicked to and fro
Across the rides between plantations
Threatening the trees, leaving a charred tread,
And signifies the ripening sun, prevents
Forest fires by homoeopathy; they say the bees
Also leave in the air tracks for their fellows
To follow, and the air is full
Of fantastic streamers like the paper pinned to the clothes;
And there are dishes passed from hand to hand untouched
Which are said to make you invisible, which may mean
    dead;

He lifts the cover; when he is tired
And ancient, he will try it; and another dish
Bears the stone that ripens
All the orchards instantly, but that is sealed.
At last that confection which procures
A vision of the Goddess going about, is served,
Which has everything, says the boy drowsily
To do with my trade, and is the caviare
Of the tramps that have no roof over their head,
Some of whom are spirits, and their feast
And their trade is to move invisibly
About the plantations and the rides
And move about them silently, leaving spoor,
And so praises to the feast that empties the house all day;
And he watches the marks the bees leave in the golden air
Under the very great light with the utterance
Proceeding from it all day echoed by the hives
And people feasting on the shores of Furnace Ponds,
Ripen, ripen.

Sue Roe

NO TAKER FOR THE SMALL SHOES

Red shoes on the ruined staircase
She swoops like a bat, comes grinning through the rafters
Lauretta! I cry, What did they say? Is it coming now?
Her laughter like Christmas Eve. The folds of her dress

My ascent is in ruins, chafes the scales from my shoulders
My shoes are in ashes, the stairs ground to powder
The spiral towards her is grazed with cracked mirrors
I reach up, she offers the folds of her dress

'They say I made a mirage again',
She sings it, surveying the hollowed decay
A butler comes scraping, his arms full of roses
She curtseys, starts putting the small shoes away.

THE SMALL SHOES (II)

Who might have inhabited the small shoes the small
red shoes tapping rhythms of russet leaf
all the way down the path to the secret garden

who might have settled in the small chair, reading
the Scriptures in miniature, listening
for murmurings of wind behind the walls

had you but entered

haunting my house with dreams of strays and fugitives
I could have unlocked the attics, unearthed
the ancient rocking horses

★   ★   ★

I heard you in the theatre at
yesterday's matinee
you stole behind the red chairs chanting
rhythms from the pantomime

but the roads to the city are cordoned off
doors bolted and chained against the late show

WRITING, AND OTHER AVENUES

Seconds before I'm due to make
My calculated entrance, timed appearance, you
Appear in dreams of doorways edged with scarlet
Testing my lines, your jacket beating behind you, your
Car keys to mark your way, and smiling, say
'You can come with me if you like.'

All the long and difficult afternoon
My papers furled and dried, the moistened nib
Poised for attack, I have sat on, revising
Your vivid entrances, dramatic
Exits, re-running previews of your absence,
Re-drafting solitude, its churchyards, its
Night-driving, roads unending and a single
Signal in the darkness: your return.
I have given it all my full attention, ranged
My colours round my palette, set my
Music to mark my hours
Hoisted my flags, prepared my
Set with the noisiest scenery.

Backstage, I'll set about repairing costumes,
Pleating notes and sketches on torn paper
And squeezed between the pages like pressed flowers, find
Memories which, succumbing to some teasing, will
Serve to mend a tear, resistingly
Yield something up: some treasure, some
Memento.

It will have been worth it, then, or so they say,
The patient afternoon time weaving shreds of
Stories' fraying fabrics, stray threads
Enraging me with their separateness, but you'd say
Keep it, don't throw anything away.

(I keep the ancient ends of all the make-up
The smallest mirrors, shattered with spilt powder,
The oldest earrings found in dark hotel rooms in
Parisian excavations masked as visits.
It makes a strange, anachronistic haul
I hide it, guard it, not throwing anything away.)

And so, at five o'clock, the dress rehearsal
The naked bulbs, the mirrors make a platform
For vivid transformations, staged constructions:
The painted face, or layers of painted faces
Superimposed, for writing is
Unpeeling, not throwing anything away.

Selecting nibs, then, and the finest pages,
I take up my position in the wings as
Dazzling in, unannounced, you make your offer.
Declining, I parade the newest costume,
Prepare my entrance, move to centre stage.

It is an empty, deathly auditorium
This world of still-unsaid, with no spectator
Your absence splinters, cold as jagged glass
(The afternoon's rehearsal was for your show)
Tomorrow reels a message out of focus:
Remembering you, and throwing you away
The staircase shifts the night air false as a straightjacket

MID-WINTER

All the crystal studded night
We tunnelled under sifting earth like amethysts
While darkness, fold on fold in silhouette,
And still no dawn, modelled its new collection.

Singly, like children's faces,
The laps of night unwrapped in waiting skies
New tones of light, like amethyst imaginings:
With brittle edge, yet flooded with magenta.

I had been here before
A million times or one, relentless time
But not like this, with night like sentinels
Ourselves like monarchs, painted, and protected.

TO SEE THE MINSTRELS

I
It was the enshrouded pier, la cathédrale engloutie, which
Put me in mind of the minstrels, its
Sunlight on frail railings, its
Water colour traces of
Suggested seascape.

Not the Palace Pier, you understand,
Posing on legs spread to withstand
The sea's violent enterings and exits,
Prince of Piers, slick survivor

The ancient one, I mean, the other
Sad one, shedding
Last fragments of corroded leaf across

The sea's vast Autumn surface,
Wise one, knowing to attend to
Whole histories of tides, their
Hot advances, soft retreats,
Remembering the old days, the
Dancing days, recalling
Its own soft-surfaced youth,
Old syncopated pier, old
Jazz-walking one,
Old soldier.

II
On one of Autumn's newly haunted days,
Slats of light taut between sea and sky but
Slowing up, now,
I took you in your new coat to the
Esplanade: you liked its name, its straightness
Showed you the ghostly pier,
Frail, wise one
Shedding its scales and salted fins
Discreetly into the rusting sea, old actor, fine
Old stager

You viewed it with suspicion, like a grandfather,
Knowing already the wile in age, its tricks
It teased you into seeing it intact,
Frosted against the ageing sky, transparent as
Castles in old stories. You asked me
Was it falling now? You could not see it fall, which bits were
        gone?
And, were there fishes swimming *right inside* it?
And what would happen one day when it fell?

(I didn't tell you that the grief that kills us
Falls piece by piece, years, peeling and corroding,
Making their strange reversals
In dreams of highly coloured, strange menageries, that
Nothing falls without first losing colour, but
Undersides of leaves in dreams are scarlet)

We waited, then, quietly at the water's edge, your
Patience for faith's sake, your
Chastity of waiting

Burned me, and the sun corroded sea salt
Into the dying light, as though to verify
The sky's staged resolution to
Sometime later, discreetly slip away.

III
You frowned ahead, then, frowning up at me . . .
I said Look now, they're coming! Watch the far end:
And on the very instant out they came.
It was a revolutionary staging,
A 'problem' staging, jagged as the late plays,
Mysterious as Satie's music: clowns on tightropes
Lauding a buried Saviour, syncopated suddenly with
Emergency stops.

Their grease paint teased the edges from the waves
As, bowing to the water's vast scenario
They staged their magic minstrel matinée
Half walking, half a mime of walking, dancing
Like old machinery, in halting imitation of
Sea-side promenades, and mockery of
Imitation.

IV
This would notate your dreams for all your life,
The minstrel dream, the vision at the sea's edge.
One day when minstrels sweep the sea of leaves
You'll see them all jazz-walking on the water
Lauding the buried pier, Old Father Time,
Soft-pedalling the salty base, its fins and scales
Stirred through with minstrel steps, and
Minstrels' laughter.

Peter Russell

FRAGMENTA QUINTILLII APOCALYPSEÔS

It's good to be mad and to know that my long hyacynthine
   hair
Falls round the naked ochre shoulders of the slave girl
Honoured this night by the wild-cat zodiac
Of my double-yoked acacia-tree bed
                  The Hyads are rising
There'll be rain enough to rinse out the acid memories
Of underhand Venetics, Pannonian editorials
And acerbic Etruscan draughts
             This girl like a Caspian eel
Darts in and out of insomniac hours
Flashing white teeth and magenta crystal in goblets
Splashed on the suède of her pampered *poppe*,
Light-brown in the mustard candle-flame
                     Life's
All scratching and bruising. Liquids and semi-consonants
Give way to affricative poses, thorns on the tongue
When the expected honey of overripe August blackberries
Turned to a bramble-crown slashes chin, chap and neck
              They say she's seen service
In luxurious Susa with Persian princes. Princesses too
She's touched with fire on undraped glistening thighs,
And given those fleshy fillies drink. Red wines
Astringent and mellow at once pour from her lips,
Satin-skinned plums and peaches ripple her torso;
Smooth golden oil drips down her arms and breasts
Losing its colour to luminous copper-bronze,
Pellucid almond and olive smeared on the walnut
Of nates and flanks lurking in violet shadows
Of late summer's Mazandaran:
            the lissom brown trout Neaira,

The fourteen-year-old goose girl who's fleeced all Corinth
Flicking a finger, tossing a tawny mane,
Poking a puce tongue out between softest cordwain lips
At the richest importers and bankers

                                        Many a time
She's changed hands like a footballer, but her tricks deft as
    ever
Set more and more gold flowing

Her hair floats in a cloud under the high canopy,
This Nausikaa of the brothels of Alexandria;
She'll crack a whip over my shoulders, across my belly,
Bite like an ermine

                              In the cold of dawn
She wraps a white fur robe around her nakedness
Letting the dark of knees
Shine through the folds

I am the sturgeon Ulysses clutching the hairy *medea*
She the lithe minnow slipping through tortuous straits

Her nails are elektron, her knuckles amber, her clove-
    crushed breath
Like a catskin folding small hands in an arch. Even so,
You'd say only magic could keep it up as she does.
Who ever heard of a common slave girl
With a god's lightning licking her finger-tips?
A goddess's bunched fireball crisped between legs
Like an April frog or a July waterboatman,
Nostrils flared like a nine-month fawn sniffing at wild
    narcissi,
Brows like black falcons, mouth crimson with quince-mush,
Breasts compact like June *cocomeri*, belly gleaming full-
    moon
Like the sorcerer's painted drum in forest shadows

How did I make her? Well may you ask,
But I'm not going to tell you, *mà Dia*, any more than I'd say
Where I find the best *cèpes* on the Pratomagno.
Valete . . .

1ST APRIL 1984

'And there shall be no more time' Apocalypse

I've planned my life in an eternity
Where every day's a life – unlimited.
Strict hours revolve the globe, and spin my bed
Around the pole, a soft cocoon for me
In which intoxicated sleep, a sea
Of instant histories, occupies my head
With all the sages and the heroes said
And did, to weave the world's entelechy.

The world's within me, quickened by the dream,
The silken hangings lull the wilful breeze
That builds the scaffold of eternity
From top to bottom, like the weaver's beam.
Ass-ears has quit his golden palaces
And stepped out into Athens glad and free.

DEVASTATION

freely adapted from Abu al-'Ala' al-Ma 'arrî (A.D. 977–1057)

Sometimes I'd like to be a stone
Frost cracks, winds hone.
The stone-breaker comes with his hammer –
I'd feel nothing, neither groan nor stammer,
Silence in time my grammar.
Spirit, if spirit be, – if lent
To a lump of clay, a heart is rent.
Body and soul, an ill-matched pair,
Each other's company can't bear.
The eternal and the fugitive
Cross on their paths. Neither will give.
The wind blows, let it blow out
This flame of life which, undevout,
Burns everything away but doubt.

Vernon Scannell

APPLE POEM

Take the apple from the bowl or bough
Or kitchen table where in gloom it glows
And you will sense, mysteriously, how
Its fragrance and substantial presence throws
A shadow shape of this one's red and green,
Whatever it may be – Rose of Bern,
Spice Pippin, Golden Russet, Hawthorn Dean –
Across the mind and then you may discern
Through every sense the quintessential fruit,
Perfected properties all apples own,
In this platonic shadow; absolute
This pleasing thing that you alone have grown.

Beneath the apple's skin, its green or gold,
Yellow, red or streaked with varied tints,
The white flesh tempts, sharp or sweet, quite cold.
Its blood is colourless; scent teases, hints
At othernesses that you can't define;
The taste of innocence, so slow to fade,
Persists like memory. This fruit is wine
And bread; is eucharistic. It has played
Its role in epics, fairy-tales, among
Most races of the earth; made prophecies
Of marriages and kept the Norse Gods young;
Shone like moons on Hesperidian trees.

And here, domestic, familiar as a pet,
Plump as your granny's cheek, prepared to be
Translated into jam or jelly, yet
It still retains a curious mystery.
Forget the holy leaves, the pagan lore

And that you munch on legends when you eat,
But see, as you crunch closer to the core
Those little pips, diminutive and neat
Containers aping tiny beetles or
Microscopic purses, little beads,
Each holding in its patient dark a store
Of apples, flowering orchards, countless seeds.

Martin Seymour-Smith

TO MY DAUGHTERS

My child (whichever) my love for you's more dear
As fatherhood becomes more clear.
Now I can no longer bear
Not to be my own ghost spying
On your mind after my dying:
Sitting in the shaft of this same sun,
Going through my dusty stuff and saying
'This was his but does not matter any more.
Nor did it ever much. Moon in Cancer,
Always he felt compelled
Crab-like to collect
Detritus of a past which now's
No longer anyone's at all,
Unless the Moon's.'

But what is never past, my child (whichever)
Is my blessing on you
As adamantine now as when I saw you first.
Love like mine for you's almost
Too much to bear
And undoes history quite.
It never can be told except
Beyond death's care, as *now*;
But then it's as heartfelt as the sun is warm.
Now, as you muse upon these relics,
Now, as I write you these words.

RACHMANINOV

Rachmaninov put his hands terribly to his head
As he found his own First Symphony
Insupportable
And at the end of the first movement
Fled,
Spent the night on a tramcar
Shuttling backwards and forwards.
It was so garish
That his mind broke down.
But it is well known
How he was hypnotised
And returned in triumph
To compose the Second Concerto.

Now I'm Rachmaninov:
Have seen all that dazzle-in-the-dark
And dark-in-the-dazzle,
Have shuttled with wrecked mind between termini,
Recovered in the sternness
Of an obdurate Russian gaze,
Rediscovered winning musical ways.

Shrunk in my firs I menace
With whistling digits
Auditoria rapturously silent
In the spirit of polite adulterous tearooms.

How do you discern my true melody?
Leave the man you were going to be guilty with,
Come to my dressing-room instead.
Though I'm a melancholy exile
I'll more than tell you what I'm like in bed.
We'll play *The Isle of the Dead*
And while you go on repeating the perfect truth
That my *Preludes* are underrated
I'll put my hands terribly to my head.

I twitch and jerk on my nerves' piano-wire
A traitor to a cursed cause self-condemned,
Nor can the obscene execution end.
Look at the evidences of desire:
At how I die, and die, bizarre metaphor
For my loveless effort to live more and more
And yet defeat my concupiscent part!

Corrupted conscience, could it be but heart:
Allow an unpled innocence to start.
But black duty's the internal saboteur
Determines the penalties I must incur –
Trapped in the passion of fanatic thought
I presided over that infamous court
And as I dance upon the cutting ligature
Watch myself on film, as ordered, to make sure
That I squirm justly in the eternal pure.

If I could only hear the animal speak
I should be spared such trials, and such defeat;
I could transform that stuprate saboteur
Into a friend who'd bind us all together
And make my heart into the thinking part.

My heart's a beast whose words come from my head
But as here I jounce, nothing can be said
Until this internal saboteur is dead:
Give me the grace at last to understand
The language of God's creatures at their end.
There's such divinity within their lack
As would give me my conversation back.

An abandoned mandolin
Lies, still unrotted, on a stone in the jungle
Where you have been, and I have not.
The wind stirs faintly its strings.

Here it is chill, the leaves scrape the ground already,
There is no mandolin,
There is sadness here because there is no mandolin,
No jungle where you have been and I have not,
Nor record of the ignorant wanderer
Who left it where he did.
But a sort of music, from my garden
Stirs faintly my stretched nerves,
My nerves which ought not to be stretched.
I cannot understand it, but,
Although my curiosity's so great,
I will not question it.
In my dreams of that mandolin
I am asking a question;
I fear the sound the wind makes in it,
I fear to understand it,
I fear to sleep, and in waking even,
Afraid, avoid all reverie.
I do not want to know why I left that mandolin
In the jungle where you have been and I have not.
I am afraid of your world.
I love you. But how can I love you perfectly?
Your knowingness is of the mandolin
And of why I left it
In the jungle where you have been and I have not.

WILDERNESS

Sweetheart, remember those small hours when time's
So infinitely stretched: a web so delicate
That only icicles define its baneful density?
It's freezing tonight, no fire will keep
Me warm, and I so long for you
That my need to hear your voice, that music
Which turns the ugly and the false back into the true –
My need to hear it aches back into the deep
Memory of what I know you know: those small hours when
    time's
So infinitely stretched: a web so delicate
That only icicles define its baneful density . . .

Since my loving begs you to lie absent and
Indifferent to my solitude, for God's mercy
Instruct me in another music: one
Whose shy power transmutes, as your heart can,
This littered and insomniac wilderness
Into a grey-blue lacustrine paradise
As quickening and as placid as your eyes.

CHRYSANTHEMUMS

Everybody's chrysanthemums,
Everybody's,
Are a good dream that will come true.
And you know as I know
From their sombre colours
Staunch against the heart-withering,
Calamitous, mind-shrinking, encumbering,
Deadening, torturing
Bleakness of weather,

That all true dreams enable,
Enable,
Love to break through.
Look now at the trees,
Stripped as if dead,
At the unbreakable ground:
Look with your battered mind's
Too consequential sadness.
Do not miss
Those reds, russets, profound dark yellows:
Late, late,
But hardy,
Perennial.

IN MY EYE

My burned stabbed single seeing eye's a cave agape
On mid-heights unscanned except perhaps
By some mad sheriff with his telescopic
Yearning to pick a rapist off. It watches you,
Empty but for some crumbling bones,
A hundred-thousand-year-old fire,
And the droppings of rabid bats.
No one civil's entered here.
I am this precipice; my eye's
Alive, though cannot glint to draw a shot
From any madman down below – and must endure
Sightless aeons of everlastingness
Like it was blind (think of the past
That's locked in me!). The lid's burned off,
Nor can tears flow: even you at times
I see through the streams that pour
Off my glacial jutting brow
Yards from my gnawed vacancy.
But there are gaps in dry eternity
When painfully I must unlearn
The secrets of the wreckage which I hold,
As when my gaze was captured by the colours

Of your bright speculations.
And you? You hardly know I watch,
Though this desolateness is yours, not mine;
I'm just the passive part of it.
You are absolute mistress,
If you could bear to take command,
Of disconsolation and the unexplored,
And of whatever lies beyond.
Thousands of miles away I see you,
Knowing you can't avoid your fate,
Handing drinks around, and laughing;
But also I see you in your sleep,
Reading your dreams from the smoke-puffs
Of the madman's rifle down below –
How could he know his frenzy's randomness
Made such a subtle pattern of your woe? –
And I watch when you're alone in sadness
And hopeful numinous imaginings.
Be aware of my charred eye, though not of me,
And of the bloody lichen running down my cheeks;
But let your dreams
And your imaginings look up still higher:
Climb this annihilated steepness
To the mottled menace of the sky above
Which can clear only in your unanguished love.

SILVERHILL

White chairs in a tall stack against a table
In the tiny garden of a pub
On a hill in sleazy St Leonards;
Greybrick houses cluster all around.
A good district to disappear into.
I watch the chairs through the window.
Are those raindrops? It's overcast,
And so am I. But nothing matches
So well my sorrow as this scene:
Last night, sunny, people had games there,
In that garden. I dwell on their small past
More keenly than they. I have a pang
At my heart, but know it's my own mind
Hurting it – that it's no longer you.
I must have wanted you to be unkind.

Walking now, I pass an entrance flanked
By two open-beaked stone birds-of-prey,
The whitewash hardly covering their grey.
A child has stuck into each mouth
A carnation ripped off just as it bloomed.
Each bird stares greyly at me from beneath
Its flakily whitened eye.
More befalls than thought, speech, action,
In the ominous air,
Like that table, that clambering top chair
Crookedly stuck into the darkening sky.

You spread that menace, but cannot care:
Play no part in this presageful fable
From which I flee – but to whom, and where?

It was as if I were widely awake
When you, half-Madonna
With child as if torn from your embrace
Said hushed and alone from a moonlit niche
'Come with me for your mind-fuck'.
We walked together upwards
Towards an unknown sky
Neither wanting from the other
Anything but warmth and sympathy.
Despite the moon I should have known
Better than to trust such luck –
I, who had never, in love, said 'fuck'.

Now it is customary day
And you are cold and shy away
From my smallest glance
And when I ask why it cannot be
In undream as in dream you say
'I don't like luck'
And are sullenly reticent.

You know you were in that dream,
But did you put yourself there,
And did you say what I heard you say?

The owl awakes from her day-long sleep
And I await the dark
Though knowing that, perplexed,
I may not find sleep.
I am thus exposed, whatever I do,
To night's inviolable deceit –
If not to a dream that is a cheat
Then to a moonlessness which hides
Your knowledge of me, your true needs,
As with closed eyes you beside me lie –
Asleep or not asleep?

W.G. Shepherd

SUBURBAN GARDEN A NATURE RESERVE

I sit pie-eyed all afternoon
In a splitting precarious deckchair
Entranced. A sparrow imbued
With rudimentary
Fieldcraft would case the lawn
From fence or twig, then swoop –
And off, out. Instead
They flutter-jump down to a spot
A mile off-target, all
Twitchy yet reckless,
And flipping their heads left right
For monocular snaps
Sneak up in hoppity zigs and zags
To pork-fat. Dimwit caution maxi-
Mizes cats' chances.

From brambles' rank thicket pads Oscar,
A gutsy slimline eunuch cat,
The black and white London Phoenician strain,
Plump finch in jaws. Easily
I persuade myself
That bird is past help. Cat juggles
With it. It resurrects, run-flying,
Four times. Cat eats it,
Crunches the beak, the Matchsticks legs,
His leavings one downy feather.

I have known a magpie
Grab, paunch and devour
A blackbird. Oscar has pulled down
A strapping

Magpie. Close-up a magpie's black
Is bright dark blue
With rainbow patina:
In bright sunlight Punic cats'
Is silver coal brown.
The white of both is white white.

Our prettily tiger-faced tabby
Columbus harries from cover
A shrew. Dropped a moment
The shrieking two-inch rodent
Rears up and bites back
At the mightily playful muzzle –
Microlite vs. Tornado. And in
Due course
The boring cadaver's forgot.

Both chaps like human companion-
Ship. I love them. Incipient
Headache. Yawn. Over N14
A kestrel watches. Owls whoop by night.
Foxes have colonised London.

THE PISS ARTIST

I ask if she is all right. She is clearly not,
And she breaks down. She complains of my chronic
        drinking.

She abhors dirty language. She describes
As 'another fucking bastard' the latest

Bottle discovered behind the waste-paper basket
Beneath my bedside table. I am not exactly

Hiding my booze. I know it will be observed.
But if it enters the house discreetly, as less than a blatant

Provocation, the odds are that she will continue
To connive at my vice, bar the occasional outburst.

In my own estimation I do not become 'drunk':
In hers drink makes me a tetchy fool – but the main

Outrage is the sheer appalling amount of money
I drink and piss out. Jack is a darling.

So pleased to be growing so fast. Apologetic
Because his feet are pinched and he needs new shoes.

She rages quietly, and cries. Then she hugs me.
I don't respond, partly because I'm not moved,

Partly in case she discovers the gin
In my anorak pocket. All I feel is anxiety

Because I feel no compassion. Registering
Her bowed head, her tears, her distorted face,

My uppermost thoughts are memories of occasions,
There must have been hundreds of them

Across the years, when she has played dumb
Rather than grant me communication . . . Sipping neat gin,

I address my Grotrian Steinweg piano and Bach's *Inventions*:
I lovingly take their counterpoint into my hands.

Col. Bascombe had in his garden a boiler.
It was impressive, though not in working order.
His friend Mr. Fotheringay fell to wondering
How much the colonel's boiler weighed.

'If you will allow me to take away your boiler,
Weigh it, and return it to your garden,
I will pay you five pounds.' The colonel accepted
This very reasonable offer.

Now in order to weigh the boiler Mr. Fotheringay
Was obliged to take it to pieces, and in pieces
He returned it. Col. Bascombe politely asked Mr.
    Fotheringay
To put his boilder together again: Mr. Fotheringay

Expressed his regret that this was not convenient.
Col. Bascombe maintained that Mr. Fotheringay
Had a clear contractual obligation to return
To the garden what he had removed from it:

The disassembled constituent parts of a boiler
Were not the same thing as a boiler.
A contract must provide for each of the parties
To receive consideration: if it does not,

It is not a contract. Mr. Fotheringay held
That he got no benefit, no consideration,
From the arrangement between himself and Col. Bascombe,
Which was not, therefore, contractually binding.

'Heaven knows what is the benefit to Mr. Fotheringay
Of knowing the weight of his friend's boiler,'
Said the judge, 'but that is not a matter for me to speculate
    upon:
The information is plainly of value to Mr. Fotheringay,

Since he has paid for it the substantial sum of five pounds.
By his own estimation he has received good consideration,
And his failure to reassemble, or have reassembled,
Col. Bascombe's boiler is a breach of contract.'

Penelope Shuttle

OUTDOOR ANNIVERSARY WITH MARIA

Indoors, I am official custodian of our museum.
Marriage only ripens outdoors, or in the greenhouse
among lazy plants with real and undisguisable names,
fuchsia, idle orchid.

Light sinks against the glass roof, a warm breath
approved by the sky lifting up its own lenient blue towers,
holding them high as the sweetheart moths;
while the tall historical stiff-bladed rushes
fringing the shallow garden pool do not move,
not even to rummage out one secret from their reflections
adorning the rusty lid of the water.

I am a wife, but I am free to punish terrestrial boys.
This garden is our planet;
here, as husband and wife, aided by interested animals,
cat and hedgehog,
we count out the autumns,
not longing for the faithless plump angels of the summer.

The en-famille of the years has taught us to shout
so that the silence of earlier journeys would seem shameless
    now
in this bronze-green garden of bracken and water-pepper,
of flowers with their aching seedheads and northerly
    perfumes,
bushes odd and sad as acquiescent machines in dreams
where the wide-awake airman flutters in his tangled strings.

In our garden-swamp of sage and fox-sedge,
we meet as searchers and collectors,

147

celebrating our wilderness marriage,
anecdotic as dogs.

Our child is named after the open-sea,
she comes towards us glowing with her emergencies,
her inch-of-rain demands.

Above her head
the day-flying moth of marriage beats its wanderers' wings,
as happy in this mock-nuptial rain and unruly garden
as it will be sad inside the house
where the craft of cushions and the art of tables
shut all three of us in, wedding-prisoners,
where our French fountain clock harnesses
us to the foam and dew of our tears,
the installments of care each room insists on,
the understudy beds we enroll in,
the sleek embassy ceilings we adopt and name,
decked in our yearly costumes as clandestine housekeepers.

THE VISION OF THE BLESSED GABRIELE

Carlo Crivelli, National Gallery, London

In the evening sky, swallows

and the saint in his robes of evening cloth
gazing upward with his worried stare.

Is it because there is no star?

His feet have slipped out of their sturdy medieval scholl
        sandals.
He kneels on hard sand where thin grasses fountain
and starfishy cacti flourish near a few egg-shaped pebbles.

The frail tree that for years has borne no plums
touches both the saint's shoulder and the sky.
He is holding his hands palm to palm,

making the old holy arch of fingers and thumbs,
his two little fingers making an exact oval.

He looks up at her as if she's a trespasser,
hanging there in her larger oval in the sky,
the queen and her babe,
as if he sees her as the queen of untruthfulness.

How worried and angrily he stares at her,
his hands kept holy and invulnerable,
his bare feet ugly and ordinary, a man's feet
on a man's earth,
behind him the barren tree
and above him, she and her fertility.

Swags of fat fruit, unbelievable ripeness, hang across the sky
supported by an old ragged linen hammock;
hanging from the sky not stars but outsize heavenly fruit
knotted in a casual arrangement of dirty bandages.

On the sandy ground his holy book lies open,
forgotten, its script of red and black abandoned
as in horror he stares up at the fruit,
apples and pears from a giant's orchard.

Who put them there, apple and pear,
growing on the same branch, fruit bigger than a child's
        head?

The hedgehoggy halo of the saint quivers.

Within this glistening vagina the sky has blurted open
like an eye or a fruit, there is this queen or golden doll
carrying her stiff golden child,
cargo lugged along by cherubs, the crumpled robe
of the woman evidence of their haste.
They peer round the edges of the mandorla, singing a
        suitable song.

And like a gulliver the helmetted man
with his thoughtful grieving head
lies face down on the path in the wood,
alive or dead, who knows?

Not the saint, still staring up at the sky with its storm of
    fruit,
at the mother of gold, her foot set on fruit,
on another goddess's golden apple.
The child holds either a second golden apple or maybe a
    golden ball.

The saint gapes. This is the pain of the answered prayer.

In the pond by Gabriele's feet, in the green water,
the drake moves to the lustrous duck
with almost unnoticed longing, with vigilant love.

On the branch of the plum tree, a bird is about to fly away,
north to China or south to India.
When the bird has flown the saint will be able to weep.

HIDE AND SEEK

The child might be hiding in the ship
or in the cave,
or in the garden where the morning-glory
will find him some pretty name;
he might be hiding in the tree
whose shed needles fall like quills
on to the pitch of the dry lawn;
he might hide in a tower
built by a father for a son who never appeared,
the son dreamed-of but never caught up
into the real photographs of life;
the boy might hide by the cat-happy door,
or find some waterfall behind which to shelter,
be shuttered-in by the sheer fall of water;
he must hide somewhere.
He is a virtual prisoner in the powerhouse of the page,
must hide from the words thumping and beating on his
    head,
but where shall he hide, this boy who has not yet learnt

how to talk like a child,
or discovered that an evasive answer is the best way
to get uninterrupted possession of your day?
He hides everywhere, primitive, prodigal,
playing any number of odd games
in the garden of the red-eyed fish, their pool of stone and
    weed,
or in the stables where three horses watch him,
startled but, like electricity at rest, intensely patient.
The child hides, underfed in his blue shirt and french
    trousers,
in the room where I expected to find anyone else but him,
even a flock of those glossy and black gregarious birds
or the stately golden sane old dog of our crazy neighbours;
butter-finger room I at once let slip away into dullness,
losing him, he is not even behind those rivals, the curtains.

The child hid in a ship
and sailed away over an ocean, beneath deep-sea stars,
into the tenderness of storms,
the tempests, the burning calms,
the retentive and temperamental weather of a child
for whom no reward was offered and to whom nothing was
    promised.

C.H. Sisson

THE HARE

I saw a hare jump across a ditch:
It came to the edge, thought, and then went over
Five feet at least over the new-cut rhine
And then away, sideways, as if thrown
– Across the field where Gordon and I walked
Talking of apples, prices and bog-oak,
Denizens of the country, were it not
That denizens do not belong, as they do
And the hare tossing herself here and there.
And I? If I could, I would go back
To where Coombe Farm stood, as Gordon's stands
Trenched in antiquity and looking out
Over immense acres not its own
And none the worse for that. You may say
It is the sick dream of an ageing man
Looking out over a past not his own.
But I say this: it is there I belong,
Or here, where the pasture squelches underfoot
And England stirs, forever to hold my bones.
You may boast of the city, I do not say
That it is not all you say it is
But at the Last Judgment it will stand
Abject before the power of this land.

WAKING

May has her beauties like another month,
Even June has her pleasures. I lie here,
The insistent thrush does not trouble me
Nor the slight breeze: a tree stump looks like a cat.
Yet all is not altogether well
Because of memory; crowd round me here
Rather, you ghosts who are to drink of Lethe.
Who else would go back to the upper world
Or take again the nerve-strings of the body
Or will to suffer grief and fear again?
Once I did: and the echo still comes back,
Not from the past only – which I could bear –
But from the young who set out hopefully
To find a bitter end where they began
And evil with the face of charity.
I have seen some such and do not want
Ever to pass along that road again
Where blind beggars hold out their hands for coin
And saints spit in their palms. This I have seen
And shall see if I wake from sleeping now.

THE VOYAGE

Happy the young man who disregards
The siren who conceals herself in words,
Stopping his ears but seizing on the flesh
Which will serve his intelligence the best:
What seas must he sail on, what strange lands
Visit before he claims to understand
What song the sirens sang or other such
Matters which do not matter overmuch.
It was not so with me: I sought to find

What errors might be in a human mind
And to embrace them all, the skimpy ghosts
Who flee like shadows when we need them most.
Yet the bold sailor comes to the same port
As I who lived on charts and false reports.
Observe the wisdom that I have today!
Which others have, who had it on the way.

LOOKING AT OLD NOTE-BOOKS

It would seem that I thought,
At that time, more than I ought;
I noted the reflections
Of those for whom perfection
Came in a sudden phrase:
How one should behave,
How others did, the wise
Remarks of men in difficulties
Or who observed others
Making a great pother
While they were easy themselves.
All this should have been useful
To a young man rising twenty,
Yet one finds that at thirty
He was still floundering.
If he understood anything
It was by way of suffering
For his first incompetence
Or third or fourth inability
To do anything sensibly.
How much had the wise helped?
They could do nothing themselves,
Being dead, buried in books
In octavo or folio, works
In several languages
And always, phrases that pleased.
What price then Schopenhauer,
Throwing a woman downstairs,

Fénelon, Proudhon,
Goethe in Eckermann
Or Plutarch in North?
I might add, 'and so forth'
– Out and around
The world but all bound
In antique leather,
Mercure de France yellow
Or the elegant brown or black
Of the *Insel-Verlag*.
There was the London Library
Doing its best to confuse me
– Then back to Valéry,
Antoine de St-Exupéry,
Barrès, Cocteau, Jouhandeau
And what d'you know?
On oriental customs,
To confirm my observations
There was the Abbé Dubois
Or the Japanese school reader
For children of five.
It can cause no surprise
That with such learning
For half an hour each morning
And a supplement at night,
I knew my way all right.
The world opened before me
Like a speck in memory,
I grew in wisdom
Like a mastodon
Or other inept animal.
Behold me now, in old age,
Seated in my cage,
Pulling through the bars
What leaves can be reached from there.
Naturally I advise
The young who would be wise
To follow my example.
They should all read examples
Of the philosophers, I recommend
The moralists of course and
The epistemologists,
There is a long list.

They are not to reject
The theologians, I expect
They will find them illuminating.
Imaginative writing
Isn't all it's cracked up to be:
Take it cautiously.
Avoid writing poems, a frequent
Cause of discontent;
You may read one occasionally
And that is all
– And all I can tell
You about how to live well.

COTIGNAC AGAIN

Cotignac is full of spies
– Not one but tells lies
Or whatever interests him;
Not one but looks out
To enquire who's about,
To mark him down and take his name.
The windows may be high, the wall
Blank, it does not matter at all:
Nothing is impervious
To the man who is callous.

Cotignac is full of thieves
– Not one but leaves
Footprints everywhere. How can
We hope to find the right man?
How believe what is said
By a man who may be dead?
How know if we are known
Or can be, by such a one?
How escape certainty
Which is of all pleasures the least?
How know what we know
When we dislike it so?

False amour where truth is found
There is none around:
The imaginary point
Puts all out of joint
– Lies, lies and lies.
So, the imaginary
Point recedes and the fact
Formerly exact
Loses reality.

Dead man, you are a lover
In the spaces of hell, either
Racketed by images
Or tendentious ghosts.
Satan in all his pride is
More complacent than most:
You mop and mow
Among the least,
Up and down, around,
Fabulously misplaced,
Erroneous, king of error,
Queen of yourself or
Mere bath-water running out:
Do you not hear the gurgle?
Follow the circle,
An ape with others, holding hands.
The supreme exit is at hand
– City of rascals, the
Infernal city
Where every inhabitant
Is imaginary.

A centre in a kingdom is absurd
You say? And where else would you find a word?
A theory, like a skein of mist that covers
The sacred members of a pair of lovers,
Mythological giants strewn by the way
Of history? The proletariat, say,
Reluctantly embraced by the middle class
Or some such dream? I at least
Prefer the ground under the two-backed beast:
Wet or fine it is less phantasmagorial,
You may even get a damp touch of the real
Or so it seems to me. Not only giants
But field-mice, rabbits, creatures more compliant
With grass and molehills – even human beings –
Shaped and sized more conveniently for doing
Whatever moles and men and women do,
Live in that terrain, having private limits
Less subject to the theoretical gimmicks
Of Marx and others living in a library.
Their words and noises are the things we see
Or hear or touch or smell, the mist that swirls
Around them is not everything in the world,
Just one delusion butting against others;
They say their piece and then their life is over.
If history rolls on they are not with it,
They understand for only half a minute
And then go blank. But the great sage Abstraction
Flies like a pteradactyl, with an action
Appropriate for imaginary millenia
Before or after there were any men here.
Here? Yes and now. Enough past for a man,
Some sunlight, moonlight, changing clouds that can
Be caught for a moment in an eye
Which must wear spectacles and then must die.

Iain Crichton Smith

THE STORY

This is the story that I've always loved.
A little girl is running towards a bridge:
she leaves her tiny footprints in the snow
and then suddenly becomes invisible.

Like the reader who leaves off reading a page,
like the dying who have still some way to go,
there are first footprints, then the unfathomable.
The Muse hasn't finished the good poem.

Perhaps it isn't good enough. Perhaps
another poem takes over, yet another
better and more invisible song will come
out of the snow with a flaring of red banners.

Perhaps one day the ending will come back.
Now we aren't finished but some day
after fresh experience we will find it,
having first tumbled from the bridge

which is a rainbow from white heaven to here.
The little girl is ageing somewhere else.
She has run through a mirror to a new country.
Drenched and flecked with snow she has changed.

What is the future? Suddenly it breaks off.
This is a sort of freedom isn't it?
Years later she appears, no more child,
but adult, and perplexed, her own mother.

Rainbow I love you, you are composed of light,
primary colours, hiatuses, a bridging.
Athlete and artist, you have perfectly curved
into the rich ignorance of the future.

THE POOR RELATIONS

Sometimes I remember the poor relations
in these huge Russian novels at the edge of
the loud action, with their threadbare gloves,
endlessly sitting in rooms while the spurred counts
stride quickly in and out. Poor relations,
no one listens to you, your voices are so faint
no one can hear you, and you sit there
in the hollow quietness like aspidistras
in their Victorian bowls. Elsewhere,
there is the noise of gunnery, oaths,
men parting tearfully with silver watches,
medallions, in the wind. The horse gulping
for air, pure air. The big book expanding
from fields where a whole class died. No,
no one listens to you. They rush out shouting
pointing at the smoke and as you wait
white carved ceilings fall and pictures melt,
countesses are rushing through the fire,
parasols over their heads.

NOT IN HEAVEN

No, it is not in heaven that we find the dry
fine winds of fact,

but in the stones of March, Holy One,
in the knots of their essence,

Galilee, wine-dark sea, miracles,
there is no miracle greater

than the literature of April,
the manuscripts of crocuses.

Shine, Holy One, from your narrow yellow niche
which has no clouds

and let me have the ambiguous dapple of April,
the sigh of a forked breeze.

IN THOSE DAYS

In those days that are called free
before I'd ever met you,
my mind was a sky without motion,
an ocean with fish that weren't mine,
and so I was forgetful
or wholly innocent of the petty
chains that may suddenly writhe like snakes
in a world where each may know the other
by the claw marks of his territory,
by his brutal and most lonely song,
his scent that hangs on barbed-wire fences.
How peasant-like the airy princes
locking their dears in rings of scythes,
lidding their thrifty treasury,
their darlings whether gold or black
wintering in their granary.

VILLAGERS

So many of those I once knew
drowned in the Atlantic or the Pacific,
that unignorable and unknown blue.

Fishermen and part-time footballers,
inadequate scholars, starers at dusty maps,
now forever locked in the sea's purse

with a miserly snap, while the guns tolled
over these restless acres not to be ploughed,
at sunset fading into a foreign gold.

These guns which defended an empire
which wasn't, isn't, yours, who have drowned
ignorantly in sharp salt and fire,

who were once big figures in the twilight
where the river gently ran and chimneys bloomed
with a smoke sometimes grey and sometimes violet,

bone of my bone, my villagers. You have met
with the foreign-spoken stranger who has pulled
you inwards to his boat, his teeming net,

a random catch, I think, not predestined,
gaping, slack-jawed, stubbly. Yet I sing
you breathless in the meshes long enchained.

Derek Stanford

IN MEMORIAM M. TAMBIMUTTU

(d. 1983)

Dying – or so one heard
so many times, these ten years back –
your actual end could not surprise or hurt
(mere routine action of time's bruising work)
save retrospectively.
      I mean, we grieve
for that wild charm and promise in its prime
when on the Lyre-bird's wings, your words
and ours (those you had chosen from our store),
took to the air; became the talk of town –
that fraction of it which discusses verse.

Bohemian wizard of the War,
you raised the means to set our songs in print.
Master of making others part with cash,
you were the high financier of our dreams;
extracting loans never to be paid back:
a fact which did not fret you over much
so long as David Gascoyne, Terence Tiller
and such gold lads lay snug between your covers.

Poetry London and those lovely cheques
redeemed the peccadilloes of your life:
the stimulants which over-stimulated,
those endless parties, bacchic hibernations,
procrastinating days, promiscuous nights.
A poet may write best on solitude:
an editor must mix more with the crowd.

You did your mixing, Tambi, without doubt.
Spoil-sports may say you somewhat over-did it.
But who are we surviving now to flout
your deep-end dolphin-like audacities.
The shy and cautious fill their days with odes
while bolder ones indulge themselves like gods;
burning up pronto.
                        Theirs a consummation
which is not quite without its violent virtue
despite the loss, the waste of flair and beauty.

Tambi, I fear the preacher's heavy touch;
and you a play-boy arbiter and Croesus,
scattering largesse freely from the purses
of well-stacked backers.
                        Oh, no call to mourn
the sovereigns of those who can afford them.
As to you, Oriental Antinous,
a last All Hail and this poor trite Farewell.

JANUS SEASON

Last week; the lawns, the sycamores
green still, their unshed clustering keys
in yellow bunches flecked with pink –
hallucinating tropic fruit.

Last week; the sun still smiting hot
exacting homage from sun-cream,
sun-hat and shorts and backless frocks;
as blue as it has ever been
this summer past; the hammering sky
nailing us supine where we lie.

This week; star-pointed foliage
face downwards on the pavement grey,
and grey the air like sullen pearls
losing their lustre in decay.

Ahead, looms time, a tunnel-mouth,
devouring deck chairs, holidays and light.

This week; the tawny silences
which only that accursed machine –
gathering leaves from eight till nine –
serves to disturb; till morning shine,
cropped grass and oyster sky grow quiet again.

October is a corridor:
that flowery door behind us shut;
but round the corner, out of sight,
another door lies just ajar,
its panels painted black and white.

A gloomy after-glow invades the room;
while fading flowers about a bed,
that's curtained close, address the ear
inaudibly: 'Step softly here.
Within lies someone who is dead.'

It is the year; and this, St. Lucy's day:
shrine of the shortest hours, the longest night.

Last week; substantial gold, the glowing Host;
but now, its epilogue and solar ghost.

Gillian Stone

MIDWINTER WARM

Something about the closing evenings of winter
That stand into the day like promontories
Each more forward than the last
Acts contrarily in a lift of spirit.

It is cold it is dark that closes, danger
Of dying before the summer or the sun.
Yet not cold or dark or danger fells
The knowledge of the warm defences.

Windows glow, Christmas is behind
The curtains. Whether the house is
Carolling or not, the staving off of cold
Counts, the deep pause in the earth throbs.

Even the man who is going to die
Comes into the light and sits,
In pain, but talking, his little breath
Claims a smile, eyes meet.

This one or that who disappears forever
Under the ribbed sea in the early night
Confirms the cold only so much as
Knowing is a warm act, itself midwinter warm.

Stefan Themerson

ENGLAND, TABLE, HAMLET, AND I . . .

England, table, Hamlet, and I
Got mixed together with minus π.
Who will manage to set them apart
Politics, logic, science, or art?

THE KING OF SWEDEN . . .

The king of Sweden who conquered Poland in the XVIIth
    century
said to the queen of England who conquered India in the
    XIXth century:
'You know, Maam, I saw a crab who was red in the sea
and green in the saucepan.
Isn't it odd. Isn't it extraordinary?'

MEANING & TRUTH

You inquire into meaning and truth
I inquire into you
he inquires into me
But meaning & truth don't inquire into him

Meaning & truth couldn't care less
and he drifts uninquired into
and drifting in his 10,000 ton heavy armour
he inquires into me
who inquire into you
who inquire into meaning and truth.

AN AMATEUR THINKS . . .

An amateur thinks
his triolet beautiful
because he broke a fingernail
on his typewriter's keyboard.

With a poet it's different,
if his poem is bad
even his broken heart
will not make it better.

WHEN I REFLECT ON NATURE'S CRUELTY

When I reflect on Nature's cruelty
am I a part of her? Because, if so,
then moral judgments are a natural thing.
And if they aren't, then how I, who hold them,
a part of her can be?

Yet, if you say, that I'm a part of Nature
   but my judgment isn't,
You say that she produces something that isn't she,
something that calls her this or that,
   for instance: 'cruel',
Yet couldn't exist without her cruelty.

P.S.: This verse, it seems, contains the gist
   of tomes of learned
   philosophy,
   but it's much easier in it to detect the twist
   of such and such
   illogicality.

   Alas, the *dis*advantage is that our great find
does not help much
so long as there's an isolated *I*
   who talks
   and talks
   and talks
about his mind.

John Wakeman

A GARDEN

On a bare tree in a garden
Hung a single wrinkled pippin.
Undeterred by time and Newton,
It clung fast to long-gone autumn.

The child who climbed there with his sorrows,
Found the tree was leafed with sparrows.
The winter sun was at his elbow,
And the light was warm and mellow.

Yet courting death, he plucked the apple,
Sunk his teeth in flesh and symbol:
It tasted, not of grief and endings,
But of wine and sun and dancing.

Far from there, in miles and years,
Despairing among cypresses,
The night scent of the alien trees,
Invoked the innocence of tears.

Then the seed that he had eaten,
Watered, came at last to season,
And it grew into a garden,
Where his wrinkled heart hung golden.

John Welch

POSTING THE LETTER

The station nameplate creaks in the wind,
Together we rise as the wrong train approaches.
That man across on the other platform
Being so caught up in his flapping clothes
Vainly grasps for his placard of title
But the words that made it up for you
Melt in your mouth and seasons blur
Into a doubtful monotone.
You don't know where you are
In this commonplace corner of town, a kind of
Enraptured drifting occurs;
The nondescript is indescribable.
It rips across, to make a rag of detail.
From nowhere, mid-afternoon, your counsel rises,
The lost novella pressing itself to a wall.

WHITE LILAC

White lilac, these restless nights
Whose heat disrupts the pages.

The nearly extinct are passing outside
You must revert to these pages.

Reggae includes itself in the leaves
The siren wails through your pages.

171

Brides of Babylon sway down the street
Pass by in carriages of music.

In sweat-shops concealed behind
Derelict Georgian façades

The machines turn all night long
Their finances enter the pages.

All this is a notion
The scent of white lilac has scattered.

Now the elderflower tips its plates towards you
Its heavy must transgressed by traffic

Floats loose over city streets.
Tonight you will sleep in their pages.

THAT NIGHT

He wrote them all down, the missing
    Fathers so large with their absence
Their dates swimming into his head
    He went to the glass-fronted book-case

And took out the piece of flayed cloth
    Its scorchings, incisions, her name
Being a snake of water
    Spoken like that from all the mouths of earth

It twisted and fell. He noticed
    Wing-beat up by the ceiling
Where it hovered in the air
    He remembered the changing her body gave him

Such a plume of love
    Together nursing unacted desires

172

Smells of the karma past. Together
    They forced open the door of light a little.

Mid-afternoon, remembers the dream
    The falling sun lights up the wall
'We make this music out of separation'
    The flower closes

'What's killed grows dense with life
    We must dream it twice in the mirror
Till one day stalking the hour
    We get closer'

He looks out onto a fallen street
    Night coming down, in all its shades
Iron or rose in the sky
    That bitter glow not rightly understood

Now he takes down the book of lightnings
    Bound in its shrivelled integument
In the brace of the neck
    A throbbing pain, suppressed angers

He and She being an act of choice
    Climbing back up to before,
As the snake, warmed, climbs
    The ladder of nerves, cellar to skull

'You and I, the skin of a dream
    Tonight, on this soil of separation.
We gaze into the face of love
    Where he sleeps on unhindered.'

Night melts in their arrival, who bring
    Wonders, the serpent
Is caught by the throat, held in the shade
    Under a cover of sleep

Not the sun itself, rising, but the moment
    Of sunrise, this fist of light, sperm
Dries on its petals
    He who burns at the door, the name of the herald

173

This brindled stone of lightnings
   Tablet of thunder, born of becoming
How it rests here now in the palm
   Gently, it does not oscillate even.

He goes upstairs
   Where his body falls back on the bed
November, twilight, alcohol and flame
   They are taking the boat to exile

He opens the glass-fronted book-case . . .

Robert Wells

BEFORE A JOURNEY

Where alders spring and a split hollow oak
Dies through hundreds of years, the quiet river
Makes slight sounds to itself like someone thinking.

The water has an unpolished silver look
At a distance. Nearby it runs transparent,
Shallow and clean over gravel with trails of weed.

Low fields, good for nothing but walking in,
Drenched grass that never dries through a winter's day:
These scenes are my whole comfort till I reach you.

THE ALFRED JEWEL

Wolf-mouth, enamelled face and golden fret:
In that fine pattern our attentions met.

I keep it from the years, our one shared day:
The little space where feeling was in play.

SUNRISE

Thin warmth toward which the body turns,
By which it grows:
                    O hardly there,

Child shot through with the first beams
Of sex, and shivering in the sun.

Hugo Williams

CALLING YOUR NAME IN THE ZOO

1. GLADYS

The would-be bride is here,
blindfold against the setting sun.
Her heart-shaped bag
has been eaten by her fiancé, the alsatian.
She is armed and smiling
as she stumbles among us with a curse.

Lighting a Greek candle, she curtsies wrongly
and ascends a ladder
let down by one of her assailants.
'Everyone wants to be me!' she cries,
as she dives out of the window
into a barrel of laughs.

2. NOELLE

If you are a fashion editor or a photographer or work
in Public Relations or advertising one of the inescapable
facts of everyday life is the constant snail's trail
of models on 'go-sees' that passes through your office.
A 'go-see' is exactly how it sounds. It can be exciting.
Girls can pick up a lot of work by being in the right place
at the right time. They can become a face overnight.
On the other hand it can be a complete waste of their time.
Sometimes when models come to see me on go-sees I realize
I must have seen them at least half a dozen times before.
On other occasions it may be a totally new, untried
fresh face that comes hesitantly through my door. Alas,
Noelle is one of the hardy perennials who has been going
on go-sees for years with very little to show for it.

When I was going through her book I asked how old she was.
She said. 'You asked me that when I came to see you last year
and when I said 24, you said "The clock's ticking on girl." '

3. ELAINE

Elaine hates touching the heads
of the older women in Giovanni's.
She has to cope with styles
that are hardly more than a few strands
clinging to bone as if nothing was wrong.
She feels desperate
until the smell of poor cooking
is drowned by the detergent.
Elaine, 17, is pregnant, but by whom?
She was doing Ruby's hair today
when it started to come away on the comb
exactly like her mother's.
'It wasn't me,' she wanted to say
when the manageress shouted at her
for spilling the dye, but the whole shop
thought how lovely Ruby's hair looked
when it came out coloured pink.
'Who's the lucky fella?' asked Ruby' husband,
putting his head round the door.
But he knew it had to be him.

Now the scissors are laid aside
and the lampshades relieved
of all the pimp-work they have had to do
on behalf of the mirrors.
The reptilian manageress
puts on the strip lighting with a frown
and switches out the sign.
Elaine, being junior, has to clear.
She feels dead, but there's nowhere to go
in this shallow lock-up
to escape the stares from the street.
She sweeps the day's clippings
into a corner, remembering a time
when she wanted to work her way up
in Giovanni's, as a colour artist.
She picks up a handful of the hair

and looks at it for a moment.
Then she throws it back on the floor.
She must hurry now
if she doesn't want Simon to see her.

4. KIRSTEN
Arching perfectly-plucked eyebrows
over blue eggshell eyes
she tells me it is possible in her country
to go all the way
from Viipuri on the Gulf of Finland
to Jisalmi, far inland,
on little steamers
which thread through channels in the rocks
and forested islands.
Moving her hand through the air
she describes how certain rivers and lakes
cascade into other lakes
in magnificcent waterfalls
which provide all the electricity for Finland.

5. TRACY & CO
You girls whose talk is all of pop,
you're showing off to us
in your halter-tops and slacks,
you're teaching us the facts
for April 1983.
Your looks announce with such mild certainty
that this is all there is
and all there ever was
of happiness in Young America.
'It's the best-in-the-world,' you say
when you stand your boyfriends up
just to be here tonight,
revolving, alone, in the spotlight.
'Try it, you'll like it,' you say.
'It's the real thing.'
When you dance in close
you turn your backs for fun:
pop heels, pop curls, pop eye shadow.
You know what's going on

is the best in the world for us.
You don't say yes just yet,
but you're fixed up for sure.
You lean towards us and say:
'Perfection would be . . .'
You say 'Purr-fection' like the disc-jockey,
flicking back your hair.
You aren't around to tell us any more.
You're moving on in Young America.

6. THEM

How perfect they are without your help,
these limited editions. How even in winter
they seem to shine when you see them,
marching ahead of you, dead set on something.
Their breasts toss things to porters, who bow.
Their knees touch as they get down into cars.
They look so interesting in their savage furs
you can't imagine their parents or their homes
or whether their beds have turn-downs.
Do they sleep, these dreams? It seems impossible
that they go willingly into darkened rooms with men,
there to make love with nothing on,
when they could be walking about in the open.
But perhaps they don't. Perhaps they are really
perched at the mirrored counter where you first saw them,
their jackets only half unbuttoned.

Here comes one now. Can you stop from reading on?
Her heels are bound in such sweet leather.
Her hair has been cut by God, regardless of the fashion.
She knows you are following her,
for she tilts you this way and that in the sun,
catching a glimpse of herself in a new hat
as she turns down Regent Street.
Did she go into Dickins and Jones?
You followed her, but she had left by the other door.
You ran out, but already she was getting into a car
when the man with a little boy came up
and asked you the way to Carnaby Street.

Jane Wilson

WILLOW IN A GALE

Sweeping the sky our willow tree has thrown
Her boneless arms with flying sleeves of leaves
Against her cyclorama with such ease
A Nureyev could be lifting and setting her down.
But she's a soloist, she doesn't care
About co-operation, she's a tree
Distracting attention from her means, a sea
Swelling and foundering upon air.

We planted this willow tree to stem the flood.
Its cells return to the clouds the tons of rain
Hoarded on our low lawn, its clay-bound
Stage. But its dancing's a bonus – our blood
Responds, elated – so long as it remains
A willow intact, with one foot on the ground.

David Wright

FOR GEORGE BARKER AT SEVENTY

I see rain falling and the leaves
Yellowing over Eden, whose
Brown waters flood below the house
Where, thirty-five years on, I live.

So long it is since first we met,
And in another world, it seems,
Where, out of pocket, down at heels,
Night after night in Rathbone Place

The kings of Poland, or nowhere,
The out of kilter, or the good
For nothings, unfit misfits who'd
Been called to follow no career,

Would find themselves, and tell the truth.
Those great originals have gone,
They're either dead or on the wagon,
Shelved in a library, or the Tate:

But, like the Abbé, you survive.
The rain has stopped, and here's the sun
Bright gold, although it's westering:
The skies clear, and the leaves alive.

ENCOUNTER IN A GLASS

Skin coarse, bird-shotted nose, the flesh loose,
Almost a hammock underneath the chin;
Eyebrows en brosse – a zareba, that one –
A sprout of hair in earhole and nostril;
Lines traversing like mountain trods the forehead:
I almost wondered who the fellow was.

I knew him well enough, the non-stranger,
And was, as despite a remembered face
You can't identify a familiar
Acquaintance in an unaccustomed place,
About to make the oddest of faux pas –
To offer him a chair and call him sir.

IMAGES FOR A PAINTER

I.m. Patrick Swift 1927–1983

I never imagined I
Should write your elegy.
I look out of the window
As you taught me to do.
All creation is grand.
Whatever is to hand
Deserves a line, praising
What is for being.
Thus at Westbourne Terrace
In long ago days
Brush in hand I'd see you
At your morning window
Transfer the thousand leaves
Of summer heavy trees
And delighting light
To another surface

Where they will not turn
With the turning season
But stay, and say
This is the mystery!
Or you would repeat
In pencil or in paint
The old stuffed pheasant too
That lived in your studio
Among the jars of turps
With a visiting ghost,
Charles Baudelaire's photo.
All the eye lights on
There for delighting.
Or put it this way,
A thing of beauty
Is joy perceived.
So you would give
Thanks for what is:
All art is praise.

Ah, those mornings
In many-hilled
Pombaline Lisbon!
The roads we travelled!
I do not mean
Only in Portugal –
Though now recalling
How, somewhere near
The river Guadiana
Going to Alcoutim,
We stopped the car
For, winding from
A muddle of brown
Round hills and bare,
Over no road came
The muleback riders
And blackshawled women
On foot, following
A coffin to nowhere:
Memento mori!

Or recollect
– Each one of us unique –

Your head suddenly
Thrown back, oblique
Eye over the laughter:
An aslant look
As if to say
Did the joke carry? The
Underlaid irony
Over the joke?

I see now
Out of my window
Mist rising from
A leaden Eden
Drifting slowly
Under trees barely
Leaved to the ford.
Gentle and aloud
The water breaks
As white as bread
Over the under road.
On the far bank

A field with trees
Each standing naked
On a fallen dress,
Brown and gold leaves.
I might relate
This season to my age.
I might relate
How swift my friend
Has gone, like these!
But I will not.
No cause for sadness,
You reader of Aquinas,
And clear Horace.
Whom the gods love, die
Young but not easily.

Biographical Details

DANNIE ABSE's autobiography, *A Poet in the Family*, was recently published in paperback by Robson Books. His *Collected Poems* was published by Hutchinson in 1977 and this was followed by *Way Out in the Centre* in 1981. A further volume of poems, *Ask the Bloody Horse*, is scheduled for publication in the Spring of 1986. He still practises part-time as a doctor and is President of the Poetry Society.

PETER ACKROYD has published two collections of poetry: *London Lickpenny* (1973) and *Country Life* (1978).

JOHN ASH Born Manchester 1948. Educated Birmingham University. Worked in Cyprus 1970–1. Toured Near East. Since then has been living in Manchester. Soon to depart for New York. Publications include: *Casino* – a long poem (Oasis Books), *The Bed and Other Poems* (Oasis 1981), *The Goodbyes* (Carcanet 1982) and *The Branching Stairs* (Carcanet 1984).

JOHN ASHBERY Born 1927 in Rochester, New York. Art critic and author – many awards and fellowships. Most recent verse publications: *As We Know*, *Shadow Train* and *A Wave*. He is currently the art critic of *Newsweek*.

ELIZABETH BAINES's short stories have appeared in a number of magazines and anthologies including *Stand*, *Encounter*, the *Literary Review* and *Firebird 3* (Penguin). Her novel *The Birth Machine* is published by The Women's Press. A second novel will be published in the Spring of 1986.

186

GEORGE BARKER Born in 1913. Educated at Marlborough Road School, Chelsea, and Regent Street Polytechnic. Married Elspeth Langlands in 1964; several children. Professor of English Literature, Imperial Tohoku University, Sendai, Japan, 1939–41; Visiting Professor, New York State University, Buffalo, 1965–6; Arts Fellow, York University, 1966–7; Visiting Professor, University of Wisconsin, Madison, 1971–2. Patron of the Poetry Society, Oxford University, 1953. Recipient: Royal Society of Literature bursary, 1950; Guinness Prize, 1962; Levinson Prize (*Poetry*, Chicago), 1965; Borestone Mountain Poetry Prize, 1967; Arts Council bursary, 1968.

ALAN BOLD was born in 1943 in Edinburgh where he attended university and trained as a journalist. He has published many books of poetry including *To Find the New*, *The State of the Nation* and a selection in *Penguin Modern Poets 15*. His *In This Corner: Selected Poems 1963–83* represents his best work over the past two decades. With the artist John Bellany he has collaborated on *A Celtic Quintet*, *Haven* and *Homage to MacDiarmid*. He has edited many anthologies.

D. BRENNAN was born and educated in the western suburbs of London but has for some years been resident in W. Australia where he is employed as a librarian.

STANLEY COOK Born 1922 at Austerfield, a South Yorkshire village. Read English at Oxford and taught in schools in Lancashire and Yorkshire; from 1969 to 1981 lectured in English Studies at Huddersfield Polytechnic. Awarded first prize in the Cheltenham Festival Poetry Competition 1972. Lives in Sheffield.

NEIL CURRY lives in Cumbria. His translations of Euripides' *The Trojan Women*, *Helen* and *The Bacchae* are published by Cambridge University Press. A collection of poems *Between Root and Sky* was published by Mandeville Press.

GLORIA EVANS DAVIES Feminist. *Words-For Blodwen, Her Name Like The Hours*, both published by Chatto & Windus. Poems have appeared in various publications including *The Oxford Book of Welsh Verse in English*, *New York Times*, *Times Literary Supplement*,

Spectator, *Listener*, *Feminist Review*, and have been featured by BBC television, radio, HTV and HTV educational pack 'Welsh Women's History'.

DICK DAVIS Born 1945 in Portsmouth. After graduating from King's College, Cambridge, he worked through his twenties and early thirties. He has published three books of poetry, a translation from Persian (*The Conference of the Birds* by Attar) done with his wife, and a critical work on Yvor Winters.

COZETTE DE CHARMOY Born London 1939. Painter and graphic artist; has exhibited widely (some eighty exhibitions in Europe, North and South America). Author of *The True Life of Sweeney Todd*, *The Colossal Lie*, *Voyages*, etc. Has contributed to various European reviews of art and poetry and has worked and travelled in Europe, North and South America. Now lives and works in the Camargue.

CAROL ANN DUFFY Born 1955, Glasgow. BA (Hons) Philosophy University of Liverpool, 1977. Poetry: *Fleshweathercock* (1974), *Fifth Last Song* (1982), *Standing Female Nude* (Anvil Press Poetry 1985). *Plays*: *Take my Husband* (1982) and *Cavern of Dreams* (1984), both produced by the Liverpool Playhouse, and *Loss* (1985 BBC Radio 3). *Awards*: C. Day Lewis Fellowship 1982–4, Eric Gregory Award 1984. Carol Ann is a full-time writer living in London and is a poetry editor on the magazine *Ambit*.

GAVIN EWART, the veteran British poet, was born in 1916. He has worked as a salesman, in advertising, and for the British Council. Now a freelance writer, his latest book *The Young Pobble's Guide to His Toes* was published in March by Hutchinson.

ALASTAIR FOWLER is a well-known critic, editor of *Paradise Lost* and author of *Kinds of Literature*. A much-travelled Glaswegian, he now divides his time between the USA and Edinburgh, where he is a professor of English Literature.His poetry includes *Catacomb Suburb* (1976) and *From the Domain of Arnheim* (1982).

GEOFFREY GRIGSON East Anglian (Norfolk) by descent, born 1905, and brought up in Cornwall, but not a Cornishman, alas. Has published anthologies and travel books; and seventeen books of verse (two volumes of collected poems), of which the latest is *Montaigne's Tower* (1984). Has lived in Wiltshire and France for more than forty years.

TONY HARRISON was born in Leeds and educated at Leeds University, where he read Classics. In 1969 he was awarded a Cholmondely Award for Poetry and the UNESCO Fellowship in Poetry and travelled to Cuba, Brazil, Senegal and The Gambia. He has published several books of poetry including *The Loiners*, which won the Geoffrey Faber Memorial Prize in 1972, and *Continuous*. He has written much dramatic verse in the form of libretti for the Metropolitan Opera, New York, and for collaborations with several leading modern composers, and verse texts for the National Theatre including *The Misanthrope* (1973), *Phaedra Britannica* (1975), *The Passion* (1977) and *The Oresteia* (1981) which was awarded the European Poetry Translation Prize in 1983.

PHILIP HOBSBAUM was born in London in 1932 and grew up in North and West Yorkshire. After attending Belle Vue Grammar School, Bradford, he won an exhibition to Downing College, Cambridge, where he read English under F. R. Leavis. He has published four collections of poems and several critical books, and is currently Titular Professor of English Literature at Glasgow University.

MICHAEL HOFMANN was born in 1957 in Freiburg, West Germany, and now lives in London. His first book of poems, *Nights in the Iron Hotel* (Faber), was published in 1983, and a second, *Acrimony*, is due out in 1986.

MICHAEL HOROVITZ started *New Departures* magazine and *Live New Departures* arts circuses in 1959, the *World's Best Jam* (of poets, musicians and poetmusicians) in 1976 and the *Poetry Olympics* (that poets of the world unite) in 1980 – all still going strong. Latest book, a nature ramble – *Midsummer Morning Jog Log*, with drawings by Peter Blake – just published by Five Seasons Press, Madley, Hereford.

ANTHONY HOWELL was born in London in April 1945 and was educated at Leighton Park, a Quaker School in Berkshire. By 1966 he was dancing with the Royal Ballet but left the ballet shortly afterwards in order to concentrate on his writings. In 1973 he was invited to the International Writers' Program in Iowa. He founded The Theatre of Mistakes in 1974, a company dedicated to poetic drama, which has performed at the Cambridge Poetry Festival and in art museums and theatres in Europe and America. His solo performances have recently been shown in Australia at the Sydney Biennale.

MICHAEL HOYLAND is a writer and painter. Besides a collection of poems called *The Bright Way In* (1984) he has had poems published in journals and magazines. He is also the author of short stories, two books on art education and a novel.

JENNY JOSEPH has published: *The Unlooked-for Season* (Scorpion 1960 – Gregory Award), *Rose in the Afternoon* (Dent 1974 – Cholmondley Award), *The Thinking Heart* (Secker and Warburg 1978), *Beyond Descartes* (Secker and Warburg 1983), *Persephone* (forth-coming from Bloodaxe); six children's books in the 1960s; selections in various anthologies; prose in magazines; occasional radio programmes.

P.J. KAVANAGH Born 1931. Has published five volumes of verse, *Selected Poems* (1982 – Poetry Book Society Recommendation), five novels and a memoir, *The Perfect Stranger*. He has also edited the *Collected Poems of Ivor Gurney*, The Bodley Head *G.K. Chesterton* and the *Oxford Book of Short Poems* (forthcoming).

JEAN HANFF KORELITZ was born in 1961 in New York and read English at Dartmouth College and Clare College, Cambridge. Her first collection, *The Properties of Breath*, will be published by Taxus Press in 1986.

B.C. LEALE was born in 1930. He lives in London where he works as a bookseller. His first two full-length collections of poems, *Leviathan* (Allison & Busby) and *The Colours of Ancient Dreams* (John Calder), were published in 1984.

190

CHRISTOPHER LOGUE, poet, playwright, scriptwriter and actor, was born in 1926. He lived in Paris for some years, where his first books were published, and returned to London in the fifties when many plays of his were produced at the Royal Court. His most recent collection of poetry is *War Music*.

GEORGE MACBETH was born in Scotland, educated in England, and now lives in Norfolk. His last book of poems was *The Long Darkness* (Secker and Warburg) and his long poem, *The Cleaver Garden*, is due out in 1986.

NORMAN MACCAIG Born 1910. Degree in Classics, Edinburgh University. Schoolteacher. Writer in Residence, Edinburgh University (1967–9); Lecturer in English Studies, Stirling University (1970–2); Reader in Poetry, Stirling University (1972–8). Married, two children – a man and a woman.

JOAN MCGAVIN is Scottish and holds degrees from the universities of Edinburgh and California. She was taught English and Creative Writing, but now concentrates on her own poetry, which has been published in various magazines. Female, liberal, humanist, Christian, she is *ipso facto* a member of four endangered species.

AGNUS MARTIN was born in 1952 in Campbeltown, Argyll. He has been writing verse since boyhood. He has had two books of social history, *The Ring-Net Fishermen* and *Kintyre: The Hidden Past*, published within the past five years, both by John Donald, Edinburgh. He works as a postman in Campbeltown.

ROBERT NYE was born in London 1939. He left school at the age of sixteen, at which time his first poems were published in the *London Magazine*. Since then he has lived by his writing, at first subsidizing his creative work by writing critical reviews in leading periodicals; he is still the poetry critic for *The Times* and a regular reviewer of new fiction for the *Guardian*. He lived for six years in a remote cottage in Wales, working on two collections of poems which won him a Gregory Award in 1963. He has since published two more books of poems, *Darker Ends* (1967) and *Divisions on a Ground* (1976). He is perhaps

191

best known for his novels: *Doubtfire* (1967), *Falstaff* (1976), *Merlin* (1978), *Faust* (1980) and *The Voyage of the Destiny* (1982). Robert Nye has been married twice, and has four children. Since 1977 he has lived in Ireland.

TOMAS O CANAINN is a lecturer in electrical engineering at University College, Cork, Ireland. He played with the Irish traditional-music group, Na Fili. He is author of *Traditional Music in Ireland* (Routledge and Kegan Paul) and his first novel, *Home to Derry*, is published by Appletree Press. He teaches uilleann pipes at the Cork School of Music.

STEPHEN PLAICE Born in Hertfordshire in 1951, he now lives in Brighton. His first collection *Rumours of Cousins* received a South East Arts Book Award in 1984. He has recently completed a second collection, *Bride of Lightning*. He is also co-translator of Ernst Bloch's *The Principle of Hope*, published by Blackwell in 1985.

SACHA RABINOVITCH Born in Egypt. Has lived in France and Italy. Translates from the French and the Italian. Has had poems published in little magazines and a collection published by Yorick Press, *Heroes and Others*, appeared in 1982.

SIMON RAE was born in 1952. After reading English and History at Kent University and doing an M. Phil, M. Litt at Oxford on Matthew Arnold and A.H. Clough he taught at Banbury School. His work has been published by the *TLS*, the *New Statesman*, the *London Magazine*, and it has appeared in various Arts Council anthologies and South East Arts anthologies. In 1981 he won a Gregory Award.

PETER REDGROVE's most recent poetry is *The Man Named East* (Routledge and Kegan Paul 1985), and also six novels or 'metaphysical thrillers' with Routledge and Kegan Paul. He is a playwright and won the Italia Prize for his radio play *Florent and the Tuxedo Millions*. He lives in Cornwall with his wife, Penelope Shuttle.

SUE ROE is the author of a novel, *Estella, Her Expectations* (Harvester 1982; paperback edition 1983). Her critical study, *Virginia Woolf, Writing and Gender*, will be published by Harvester in 1986. She is the editor of a collection of critical work entitled *Women Reading Women's Writing*, which will also appear from Harvester in 1986. She is now completing a second novel.

PETER RUSSELL, British, of Irish descent, born 1921. Artillery service in Europe and Burma 1939–46. Edited *Nine* review (1949–56) and *An Examination of Ezra Pound* (1949). Student of classical, Slavonic and Oriental languages and philosophy. *Inter alia* has published *The Elegies of Quintilius, The Golden Chain, Elemental Discourses, Selected Poems* (Anvil 1984). Lives in Italy with wife and three children.

VERNON SCANNELL Born 1922. Served in Second World War – Middle East and Normandy with Gordon Highlanders. Former amateur and professional boxer. Has won the Heinemann Award and the Cholmondeley Poetry Prize for his poetry. Most recent publications *Collected Poems* (1980); *Winterlude, Poems* (1982); *Ring of Truth*, a novel (1983).

MARTIN SEYMOUR-SMITH was born in 1928 in Stoke Newington. He has written over thirty books, among which the best known are the pioneering old-spelling edition of Shakespeare's *Sonnets*, the biography of Robert Graves and the *Guide to Modern World Literature*, now enlarged and revised as the *Macmillan Guide to World Literature*. He plans to publish his new collection of poems, *The Internal Saboteur*, in the near future.

W.G. SHEPHERD was born in 1935 and educated at Brentwood School and Jesus College, Cambridge, where he read the English tripos. He lives in London and works in industry. Three collections of his poems have been published by Anvil Press, and his translations of Horace and Propertius are Penguin Classics.

PENELOPE SHUTTLE's poetry has appeared in numerous magazines and anthologies, most recently in *The Penguin Book of Contemporary British Poetry* and *No Holds Barred*. Her two collections of poetry are

The Orchard Upstairs (1980) and *The Child-Stealer* (1983). She is married to Peter Redgrove and has a young daughter.

C.H. SISSON Born 1914 in Bristol. Educated at the University of Bristol and in France and Germany. Worked for years in the Ministry of Labour. Now lives in Somerset. A score of books to his credit or discredit. *Collected Poems 1943–83* (Carcanet Press) published in 1984. New translation of the *Aeneid* to appear in 1986.

IAIN CRICHTON SMITH Born 1928 in the Island of Lewis. Bilingual, writing in English and Gaelic; has written about fifty books – novels, poetry, short stories – in both languages. Freelance writer. Married. Latest novel *The Tenement* (Gollancz). Latest collection of poems *Selected Poems* (Carcanet). The previous collection *The Exiles* (Carcanet) was a Poetry Society Choice.

DEREK STANFORD was born in 1918 in a near Thames-side suburb of western London. After war service, he kept himself afloat by authorship, reviewing and conducting poetry classes. He is a *fin-de-siècle* enthusiast, and has written many volumes on the 1890s. He published a critical anthology, *Beardsley's Erotic Universe*, in 1967 and his 800-line poem, *The Vision and Death of Aubrey Beardsley*, is appearing with Redcliffe Press later this year. His *Pre-Raphaelite Writing* is published by Everyman; and Southern Arts Association granted him a bursary to write the long poem: *Pre-Raphaelites: The Secret Life*.

GILLIAN STONE Antiquarian bookseller. Broadcast on BBC 3 and Scottish service. Published in *New Yorker*, *Scotsman*, *Tribune*, *Countryman*, etc. Collections: *Snaily House* (Cock Robin Press 1975) and *Protection Racket* (Keepsake Press 1982). Her first full-length collection, *Survivor in a Black Coat*, is forthcoming shortly from Taxus. Born in Mauritius, educated in Jerusalem and at Edinburgh University, where she read Geography. Has lived in Teddington, St Andrews and Devon. Has brought up a family; now lives and sells books with husband in Oxford.

STEPHEN THEMERSON Born 1910. His books include *Dno Nieba* (1943); *Croquis dans les Ténèbres* (1944); *Bayamus or the Theatre of Semantic Poetry* (1949); *Wooff Wooff* (1951); *Professor Mmaa's Lecture* (1953); *factor T* (1956); *Cardinal Pölätüo* (1961); *Tom Harris* (1967); *St Francis and the Wolf of Gubbio* (an opera, 1972); *Special Branch* (1972); *Logic Labels and Flesh* (1974); *On Semantic Poetry* (1975); *General Piesc* (1976); *The Chair of Decency* (1981); *The Urge to Create Visions* (1983); *The Mystery of the Sardine* (1985).

JOHN WAKEMAN was born in London, worked as a librarian in London and Brooklyn, and now lives in Norwich. He edits reference books for an American publisher (*World Authors*, etc.), and helps to edit a poetry magazine, *The Rialto*. A pamphlet of poems, *A Sea Family*, appeared in 1980 and a larger collection, *A Room for Doubt*, is due from Taxus this year.

JOHN WELCH was born in 1942 and lives in London. His most recent collection of poetry *Out Walking* was published by Anvil in 1984. Since 1975 he has run The Many Press which publishes books and pamphlets of new poetry, and a critical magazine *The Many Review*.

ROBERT WELLS Born 1947 in Oxford. Author of *The Winter's Task* (poems), Carcanet (1977) and a verse translation of Virgil's *Georgics*, Carcanet (1982). His *Selected Poems* and a translation of the *Idylls* of Theocritus are forthcoming.

HUGO WILLIAMS was born in 1942. He has written several books of poems, of which the last two have been *Love-Life* (1980) and *Writing Home* (1985). He has also written two travel books, one called *No Particular Place to Go*. He is the television critic and poetry editor on the *New Statesman*.

JANE WILSON Born in Hampshire; grandmother of two Northumbrians. Writes plays, articles and stories as well as poetry. Four composers have set her work to music, and she is now collaborating on an opera, *A Sum Of Loves*, with Barry Seaman.

DAVID WRIGHT Educated at Northampton School for the Deaf and Oriel College, Oxford. B.A. Staff of the *Sunday Times* 1942–7. Editor *Nimbus* 1955–6. Atlantic Award in Literature 1956. Gregory Fellow in Poetry, University of Leeds, 1965–7. Fellow of the Royal Society of Literature 1966. Guinness Poetry Prizes 1958–60.